EXPRESS.

JS

FOR

BEGINNERS

A Complete Guide to Web Development with Node.js, JavaScript, and REST APIs

BY

Jason Steven

Table of Contents

Contents

PART 1: GETTING STARTED WITH EXPRESS.JS

Chapter 1: Introduction to Express.js

1.1 What is Express.js?

Web development has come a long way. In the early days, developers had to manually manage servers, handle HTTP requests, and build everything from scratch. As the complexity of web applications grew, frameworks emerged to simplify development. Express.js is one such framework—minimal, flexible, and powerful.

Express.js, or simply Express, is a fast, unopinionated, and lightweight web framework for Node.js. It provides a thin layer of fundamental web application features while keeping the core functionality of Node.js intact. This means developers can build robust APIs, web applications, and microservices without the overhead of a full-fledged framework.

At its core, Express is designed to handle HTTP requests and responses efficiently, making it ideal for building RESTful APIs and dynamic web applications. It abstracts much of the complexity involved in setting up a web server with Node.js, allowing developers to focus on writing application logic instead of reinventing the wheel.

A simple Express server can be created with just a few lines of JavaScript:

JavaScript – Setting Up a Basic Express Server

javascript

```javascript
const express = require('express');

const app = express();


app.get('/', (req, res) => {

    res.send('Hello, World!');

});

app.listen(3000, () => {

    console.log('Server    is    running    on
http://localhost:3000');

});
```

This minimal example demonstrates how Express makes it easy to handle requests and send responses. In just a few lines, we have a working server listening on port 3000.

1.2 Why Use Express.js for Web Development?

With many frameworks available for building web applications, why should developers choose Express.js? The answer lies in its **simplicity, flexibility, and performance.**

Minimalistic Yet Powerful

Unlike some frameworks that impose strict structures and conventions, Express is unopinionated. This means developers have full control over how they structure their applications. Whether building a small API or a large-scale application, Express provides the essential tools without unnecessary complexity.

Middleware System

One of Express's greatest strengths is its middleware system. Middleware functions are used to process requests before they reach the final handler, enabling features such as authentication, logging, and request parsing. This modular approach makes it easy to extend functionality without bloating the core application.

Example of middleware usage:

javascript

```javascript
app.use((req, res, next) => {

    console.log(`${req.method} request for ${req.url}`);

    next();

});
```

This middleware logs every incoming request before passing control to the next function.

Asynchronous and Non-Blocking

Since Express is built on top of Node.js, it benefits from its asynchronous and non-blocking architecture. This allows it to handle multiple requests simultaneously, making it well-suited for high-performance applications.

Large Ecosystem and Community Support

Express has a vast ecosystem of third-party libraries and middleware that can be easily integrated. Whether you need authentication, database connectivity, or caching, there's likely an Express-compatible package available.

1.3 Understanding the Role of Node.js and JavaScript in Express.js

To fully grasp Express.js, it's important to understand the relationship between Node.js and JavaScript.

JavaScript Beyond the Browser

Traditionally, JavaScript was confined to the browser. However, with the introduction of Node.js, JavaScript can now run on the server. Node.js is a runtime environment that enables JavaScript to execute outside the browser, allowing developers to build backend services, APIs, and real-time applications.

Event-Driven, Non-Blocking Architecture

Node.js operates on an event-driven model, which means it can handle multiple requests efficiently without blocking execution. This is a key reason why Express.js is so performant—it leverages Node's event loop to handle concurrent requests seamlessly.

Example: Handling multiple requests asynchronously in Express:

javascript

```
app.get('/data', async (req, res) => {

    const       data       =       await
fetchDataFromDatabase();

    res.json(data);

});
```

By using asynchronous programming, Express ensures that long-running operations (such as database queries) do not block other requests.

1.4 Key Features and Advantages of Express.js

Express.js provides a range of features that simplify web development while maintaining flexibility.

1. Routing System

Express offers a simple yet powerful routing system, allowing developers to define endpoints for handling different HTTP requests.

javascript

```javascript
app.get('/users', (req, res) => {

    res.send('List of users');

});
```

Routes can also include parameters and query strings for dynamic behavior.

2. Middleware Support

Middleware functions enable Express applications to process requests before sending a response. Common middleware includes:

- **Body parsing** (handling JSON or form data)

- **Authentication and authorization**

- **Logging and error handling**

javascript

```javascript
const bodyParser = require('body-parser');

app.use(bodyParser.json());
```

3. Template Engine Support

Express supports template engines like EJS, Pug, and Handlebars for rendering dynamic HTML pages.

javascript

```javascript
app.set('view engine', 'ejs');
```

4. RESTful API Development

Express is commonly used to build RESTful APIs, making it easy to create scalable and maintainable services.

javascript

```javascript
app.post('/create-user', (req, res) => {

    const user = req.body;

    res.status(201).json({    message:    'User
created', user });

});
```

5. Error Handling

Express provides robust error handling mechanisms, allowing developers to manage exceptions gracefully.

javascript

```javascript
app.use((err, req, res, next) => {

    console.error(err.stack);
```

```
    res.status(500).send('Something          went
wrong!');

});
```

Express.js is a powerful yet lightweight framework that simplifies web development with Node.js. Its unopinionated nature allows developers to structure applications as needed while offering a robust set of features for handling routing, middleware, error management, and API development.

By understanding the role of Node.js and JavaScript, developers can leverage Express to build scalable, high-performance applications. As we move forward in this book, we will explore practical implementations, best practices, and real-world use cases that will help you master Express.js.

Chapter 2: Setting Up the Development Environment

Web development is as much about writing code as it is about setting up the right environment. A well-configured setup can save hours of debugging, improve productivity, and make the development process seamless. In this chapter, we'll walk through installing Node.js, setting up an Express.js project, understanding package management, and equipping ourselves with essential developer tools.

Many developers, especially beginners, struggle with the initial setup—not because it's inherently difficult, but because small misconfigurations can lead to frustrating errors down the line. This chapter aims to ensure you start with a solid foundation, so by the time you write your first Express application, everything works smoothly.

2.1 Installing Node.js and npm

Web development today demands speed, efficiency, and flexibility. Express.js provides exactly that, but before diving into it, there's one crucial prerequisite—**Node.js**. Without Node.js, Express.js wouldn't exist. It's the backbone that enables JavaScript to run on the server, making it possible to build full-stack applications using a single programming language.

Imagine you're setting up a new development machine. You're eager to start building web applications, but you need the right tools first. Just like a carpenter wouldn't start a project without a hammer and saw, a JavaScript developer working with Express.js needs **Node.js** and **npm (Node Package Manager)** to get started.

Understanding Node.js and npm

What is Node.js?

Node.js is a **runtime environment** that allows JavaScript to execute outside the browser. Unlike traditional JavaScript, which is confined to running in a web browser, Node.js enables developers to use JavaScript to build server-side applications.

It's built on **Chrome's V8 engine**, the same engine that powers Google Chrome's JavaScript execution. The key advantage? Speed. Node.js compiles JavaScript into highly optimized machine code, making it incredibly fast.

Why Does Express.js Depend on Node.js?

Express.js is a **framework** built on top of Node.js, which means it leverages Node's features to handle HTTP requests, manage middleware, and create APIs efficiently. Without Node.js, you wouldn't be able to install or run Express.js applications.

What is npm?

npm (Node Package Manager) is a tool that helps developers manage **third-party libraries** and **dependencies** for Node.js applications. It's the largest package registry in the world, containing thousands of open-source JavaScript libraries, including Express.js.

With npm, you can:

- Install and manage libraries like Express.js, MongoDB drivers, and authentication tools.

- Automate tasks such as running scripts or handling dependencies.

- Keep track of project configurations and dependencies via `package.json`.

Now that we understand why Node.js and npm are essential, let's install them.

Installing Node.js and npm

Step 1: Download and Install Node.js

1. **Visit the Node.js website**: Go to https://nodejs.org.

2. **Choose the correct version**:

   ○ Download the **LTS (Long-Term Support)** version. LTS versions are stable and recommended for most development projects.

   ○ Avoid the latest "Current" version unless you specifically need new experimental features.

3. **Run the installer**:

- Open the downloaded file and follow the installation prompts.

- Make sure to check the box that says **"Add to PATH"** (on Windows) so you can run Node.js from any terminal.

Step 2: Verify the Installation

After installation, open a terminal or command prompt and run the following commands to check if Node.js and npm are properly installed:

sh

```
node -v
```

This should display the installed version of Node.js.

sh

```
npm -v
```

This should display the installed version of npm.

If both commands return version numbers, Node.js and npm are successfully installed.

Alternative Installation Methods

If you need more control over your Node.js versions or want to switch between multiple versions, consider using **Node Version Manager (nvm)**.

Installing Node.js via nvm (Recommended for Developers)

`nvm` (Node Version Manager) allows you to install and switch between different versions of Node.js. This is useful when working on projects that require specific Node versions.

Installing nvm on macOS/Linux

Run the following command in your terminal:

sh

```
curl                                          -fsSL
https://raw.githubusercontent.com/nvm-
sh/nvm/v0.39.4/install.sh | bash
```

Then, restart your terminal and verify the installation:

sh

```
nvm --version
```

Installing nvm on Windows

Windows users should install **nvm-windows** from https://github.com/coreybutler/nvm-windows/releases.

Once installed, restart the terminal and run:

sh

```
nvm install 18
```

21

```sh
nvm use 18
```

This installs and sets Node.js 18 as the active version.

Using `nvm`, you can switch between Node.js versions anytime:

sh

```sh
nvm use 16
```

Common Installation Issues and Fixes

1. "Command not found" error when running `node -v` or `npm -v`

- Ensure Node.js is properly installed and added to your system's PATH.

- Restart your terminal or reboot your machine.

2. npm Permission Issues on macOS/Linux

If you encounter errors when installing packages globally, use the following command to fix npm permissions:

sh

```sh
sudo chown -R $(whoami) ~/.npm
```

3. Running the Wrong Version of Node.js

If you installed Node.js manually but still see an old version, check your PATH settings or use `nvm` to manage versions.

Best Practices After Installation

Once Node.js and npm are installed, follow these best practices to ensure a smooth development experience:

1. **Keep Node.js Updated**

   - Regularly update Node.js to receive security patches and performance improvements.

   - Use `nvm install latest` to always stay up-to-date.

2. **Use npm Scripts Instead of Global Installs**

   - Instead of running global installs (`npm install -g package`), define scripts in `package.json` to maintain consistency across environments.

3. **Check npm Security Vulnerabilities**

   - Run `npm audit` to check for vulnerabilities in installed packages.

4. **Use `npx` for One-Time Commands**

Instead of installing CLI tools globally, use `npx`. Example:

sh

```
npx create-react-app my-project
```

- ○
- ○ This runs the package without installing it permanently.

2.2 Setting Up an Express.js Project Step by Step

You've installed Node.js and npm. Now, it's time to put them to work. Setting up an Express.js project is the first step toward building real-world web applications. Whether you're building a simple REST API or a full-fledged web app, a well-structured Express.js setup ensures scalability, maintainability, and efficiency.

Imagine you're working on a new project—maybe a backend for a to-do list app, a blog, or an API that serves data to a mobile app. You need a lightweight yet powerful framework to handle routes, process requests, and connect to a database. This is exactly where Express.js shines.

In this chapter, we'll walk through setting up a clean Express.js project, ensuring best practices from the start. You won't just install Express and call it a day; you'll learn the reasoning behind each step, setting a strong foundation for future development.

Why a Proper Project Setup Matters

Many developers jump straight into writing code without considering the structure of their application. While this might work for quick experiments, it often leads to messy, unmaintainable code in real-world projects. A well-structured Express.js project:

- **Keeps code organized** – Making it easier to navigate and scale.

- **Separates concerns** – Preventing a single file from becoming a tangled mess.

- **Enhances maintainability** – Allowing multiple developers to collaborate smoothly.

- **Improves debugging** – Making it easier to pinpoint issues.

By the end of this chapter, you'll have a properly structured Express.js project, ready for real-world development.

Step 1: Create a New Project Directory

First, navigate to a directory where you want to set up your Express.js project. Open a terminal and run:

sh

```
mkdir express-app

cd express-app
```

This creates a new folder named `express-app` and moves into it.

Step 2: Initialize a `package.json` File

Every Node.js project needs a `package.json` file. This file:

- Tracks dependencies (like Express.js).

- Stores metadata about your project (name, version, scripts).

- Helps in project configuration and automation.

To initialize it, run:

sh

```sh
npm init -y
```

The `-y` flag automatically fills default values, creating a `package.json` file like this:

json

```json
{

  "name": "express-app",

  "version": "1.0.0",

  "description": "",
```

```
  "main": "index.js",

  "scripts": {

    "test": "echo \"Error: no test specified\"
&& exit 1"

  },

  "dependencies": {},

  "devDependencies": {},

  "author": "",

  "license": "ISC"

}
```

While this is just a starting point, it's a crucial step toward a well-organized project.

Step 3: Install Express.js

Now, install Express.js as a dependency:

sh

```
npm install express
```

This downloads Express and adds it to dependencies in package.json:

json

```
"dependencies": {

  "express": "^4.18.2"

}
```

If you ever need to reinstall dependencies (on another machine, for example), running npm install will fetch everything listed in package.json.

Step 4: Create the Entry Point (index.js)

In the project directory, create a file named index.js. This will serve as the entry point of your application.

sh

```
touch index.js   # macOS/Linux

echo > index.js   # Windows
```

Now, open index.js in a code editor and set up a basic Express server:

javascript

```javascript
// Import the Express module

const express = require("express");

// Create an Express application

const app = express();
```

```javascript
// Define a port number

const PORT = process.env.PORT || 3000;

// Define a basic route

app.get("/", (req, res) => {

    res.send("Hello, Express!");

});


// Start the server

app.listen(PORT, () => {

    console.log(`Server    is    running    on
http://localhost:${PORT}`);

});
```

Understanding the Code

- **Importing Express** – The first line imports Express.js.

- **Creating an app instance** – This initializes the Express application.

- **Defining a port** – The app will run on port 3000 (or any port specified in process.env.PORT).

- **Setting up a route** – The `app.get()` method defines a route that responds with `"Hello, Express!"` when accessed.

- **Starting the server** – The `app.listen()` method starts the server, logging a message to the console.

Step 5: Run the Server

To start your Express.js application, run:

sh

```
node index.js
```

If everything is set up correctly, you should see:

arduino

```
Server is running on http://localhost:3000
```

Now, open a browser and visit `http://localhost:3000`. You should see:

```
Hello, Express!
```

Congratulations! You've just set up a basic Express.js server.

Step 6: Install Nodemon for Automatic Restarting

Restarting the server manually every time you make a change is inefficient. **Nodemon** is a tool that automatically restarts your server whenever you modify files.

Install it as a development dependency:

sh

```sh
npm install --save-dev nodemon
```

Now, update the scripts section of package.json:

json

```json
"scripts": {
  "start": "node index.js",
  "dev": "nodemon index.js"
}
```

Run the server using:

sh

```sh
npm run dev
```

Now, Nodemon watches for file changes and restarts the server automatically.

Step 7: Organizing the Project Structure

Right now, everything is inside `index.js`, but as your app grows, you'll want a structured approach. A common pattern for Express.js projects looks like this:

php

```
express-app/

|── node_modules/      # Installed dependencies

|── public/            # Static files (CSS, JS, images)

|── routes/            # Route handlers

|── views/             # Template files (if using a templating
engine)

|── index.js           # Entry point

|── package.json       # Project metadata

|── .gitignore         # Files to ignore in version control
```

For example, instead of defining all routes in `index.js`, you can create a `routes` folder:

```
routes/

|── users.js
```

|— products.js

Then, in `index.js`, import and use these route files:

javascript

```javascript
const userRoutes = require("./routes/users");
app.use("/users", userRoutes);
```

This keeps your app modular and easier to manage.

Common Issues and Debugging Tips

Issue: "Port Already in Use" Error

If you see an error like this:

perl

```
Error: listen EADDRINUSE: address already in
use :::3000
```

It means another process is already using port 3000. Either:

Kill the process using:

sh

```sh
lsof -i :3000   # macOS/Linux

netstat -ano | findstr :3000   # Windows
```

-

- Change the port number in `index.js`.

Issue: "Module Not Found"

If `express` is missing:

- Ensure you ran `npm install express`.

Delete `node_modules` and `package-lock.json`, then reinstall:

```sh
rm -rf node_modules package-lock.json

npm install
```

2.3 Understanding package.json and npm Packages

Imagine you've just inherited a Node.js project from another developer. You clone the repository, open the folder, and see a single file named `package.json`. This file is the heart of the project, telling you everything you need to know—what dependencies are installed, what scripts can be run, and even some metadata about the application.

But what if it's missing? How do you set up a project from scratch? Or worse, what if it's bloated with unnecessary packages, slowing down the development process?

Understanding package.json and npm (Node Package Manager) is critical for managing any Node.js or Express.js project efficiently. In this chapter, we'll break down how package.json works, explore npm packages, and discuss best practices for handling dependencies.

Why package.json Matters

The package.json file is more than just a list of dependencies. It serves several key roles in an Express.js project:

- **Dependency Management** – Keeps track of the packages your project needs.

- **Project Metadata** – Contains essential details like the project name, version, and description.

- **Scripts for Automation** – Defines commands for running, testing, and deploying applications.

- **Version Control for Dependencies** – Ensures consistency across different environments.

Without package.json, sharing or deploying an Express.js project would be chaotic. Imagine sending an entire node_modules folder (which can be hundreds of megabytes) instead of just listing the required packages.

Creating a package.json File

If you haven't already set up a `package.json` file, you can generate one by running:

sh

```sh
npm init -y
```

This command creates a `package.json` file with default values. Here's what it might look like:

json

```json
{
  "name": "express-app",
  "version": "1.0.0",
  "description": "",
  "main": "index.js",
  "scripts": {
    "test": "echo \"Error: no test specified\" && exit 1"
  },
  "dependencies": {},
  "devDependencies": {},
  "author": "",
  "license": "ISC"
```

```
}
```

Let's break this down.

Key Fields in `package.json`

1. Project Metadata

These fields describe the project:

- `name` – The project's name.

- `version` – The current version, following Semantic Versioning (`major.minor.patch`).

- `description` – A short summary of what the project does.

- `author` – The creator's name (optional).

- `license` – Specifies how the code can be used.

These fields help organize and document your project, especially when working in teams.

2. `dependencies` **vs.** `devDependencies`

Dependencies (`dependencies` **)**

These are packages required for your application to run. For example, installing Express adds it here:

sh

```
npm install express
```

`package.json` updates automatically:

json

```json
"dependencies": {
  "express": "^4.18.2"
}
```

Development Dependencies (`devDependencies`)

These packages are only needed during development (not in production). Common examples include:

sh

```sh
npm install --save-dev nodemon eslint
```

This updates `package.json` as:

json

```json
"devDependencies": {
  "nodemon": "^3.0.0",
  "eslint": "^8.50.0"
}
```

Rule of Thumb:

- Use `dependencies` for libraries your app needs to run (e.g., Express, database drivers).

- Use `devDependencies` for tools used in development (e.g., testing frameworks, linters).

Understanding npm Packages and Versioning

When installing a package, npm assigns it a version following **Semantic Versioning (SemVer)**:

```
major.minor.patch
```

Example:

```
4.18.2
```

- **Major (4)** – Breaking changes that might require modifying your code.

- **Minor (18)** – New features added but still compatible with previous versions.

- **Patch (2)** – Bug fixes or small improvements.

You might see symbols like ^ or ~ in `package.json`:

- `^4.18.2` – Updates to the latest minor and patch versions (e.g., `4.19.0` but not `5.0.0`).

- ~4.18.2 – Updates only to the latest patch version (e.g., 4.18.5 but not 4.19.0).

To lock a package at an exact version, remove the ^ or ~.

Managing npm Packages

1. Installing Packages

To install a package, use:

sh

```
npm install package-name
```

For example:

sh

```
npm install express
```

2. Uninstalling Packages

If you no longer need a package:

sh

```
npm uninstall express
```

This removes it from `package.json` and `node_modules`.

3. Updating Packages

To check outdated packages:

sh

```
npm outdated
```

To update all packages:

sh

```
npm update
```

If a package has a major version update, manually install the new version:

sh

```
npm install express@latest
```

Using npm Scripts

Scripts in `package.json` automate tasks. The default `test` script looks like this:

json

```
"scripts": {

  "test": "echo \"Error: no test specified\"
&& exit 1"

}
```

You can customize it. For example, to run an Express server with Nodemon:

json

```
"scripts": {

  "start": "node index.js",

  "dev": "nodemon index.js"

}
```

Now, start the server using:

sh

```
npm run dev
```

Common Issues and Debugging Tips

1. "Module Not Found" Error

If you see:

javascript

```
Error: Cannot find module 'express'
```

Try:

sh

```
npm install
```

If it persists, delete `node_modules` and `package-lock.json`, then reinstall:

sh

```
rm -rf node_modules package-lock.json
npm install
```

2. "Version Mismatch" Issues

If a package update breaks your project, check which versions you've installed:

sh

```
npm list express
```

To revert to a previous version:

sh

```
npm install express@4.18.2
```

2.4 Essential Developer Tools and Debugging Techniques

Introduction

Every developer, no matter their experience level, has faced the frustration of a bug that just won't go away. You've written what seems like flawless Express.js code, but for some reason, your API is returning a `500 Internal Server Error`, or maybe it's just stuck with no response at all.

Welcome to the reality of web development—where debugging is just as important as writing code. The good news? The right tools and techniques can turn debugging from a nightmare into a structured process.

In this chapter, we'll explore essential tools that streamline development and debugging, from logging requests with Morgan to stepping through code with the Node.js debugger. More importantly, we'll discuss practical debugging techniques that will save you hours of frustration.

Must-Have Developer Tools for Express.js

Before diving into debugging techniques, let's cover a few tools that will enhance your Express.js development workflow.

1. Nodemon – Automatic Server Restarts

By default, when you make changes to your Express.js application, you have to manually stop and restart the server for those changes to take effect. That's tedious.

Enter **Nodemon**, a tool that automatically restarts your server whenever you modify your files.

Installing Nodemon

sh

```
npm install --save-dev nodemon
```

Then, update the scripts section of package.json:

json

```
"scripts": {
  "start": "node index.js",
  "dev": "nodemon index.js"
}
```

Now, instead of running:

sh

```
node index.js
```

Use:

sh

```
npm run dev
```

Your server will restart automatically every time you save a file.

---

2. Morgan – Request Logging Made Easy

Debugging an Express.js app often starts with understanding what requests are coming in. **Morgan** is a simple HTTP request logger that helps you track incoming requests, status codes, and response times.

Installing Morgan

sh

```
npm install morgan
```

Using Morgan in an Express App

javascript

```javascript
const express = require("express");

const morgan = require("morgan");

const app = express();
```

```
// Log all requests to the console

app.use(morgan("dev"));


app.get("/", (req, res) => {

  res.send("Hello, world!");

});

app.listen(3000, () => {

  console.log("Server running on port 3000");

});
```

Now, every request to your server will be logged in the console:

sql

```
GET / 200 7.234 ms - 13
```

Morgan is invaluable for tracking unexpected requests, debugging routes, and analyzing API usage.

---

3. Postman – API Testing Without the Guesswork

When building Express APIs, you don't always have a frontend ready to test endpoints. **Postman** allows you to manually send requests, view responses, and debug API behavior.

With Postman, you can:

- Send GET, POST, PUT, and DELETE requests.

- Inspect headers, status codes, and response bodies.

- Automate API testing with collections and scripts.

If an API call isn't behaving as expected, Postman lets you inspect request payloads, verify response data, and debug authentication issues.

4. Debugging with Chrome DevTools and Node.js

Node.js provides built-in debugging support through the inspect flag. You can use Chrome DevTools to set breakpoints and inspect your Express.js code.

Running the Node.js Debugger

Start your Express server in debug mode:

sh

```
node --inspect-brk index.js
```

Then, open Chrome and visit:

48

arduino

```
chrome://inspect
```

Click **"Open dedicated DevTools for Node"**, and you'll be able to set breakpoints, step through your code, and analyze variables in real time.

Practical Debugging Techniques

Now that we have our tools set up, let's go over real-world debugging techniques that will help you identify and fix issues faster.

1. Debugging Server Crashes

A common issue in Express apps is the dreaded **"server crashes unexpectedly"** problem. The best way to debug this is to wrap asynchronous code in proper error handling.

Example: Unhandled Rejection

Consider this problematic route:

javascript

```
app.get("/user/:id", async (req, res) => {

  const         user         =         await
getUserById(req.params.id); // If this fails,
the app crashes
```

```
  res.json(user);

});
```

If `getUserById` throws an error, the app will crash. The fix? Always use `try...catch` in asynchronous functions:

javascript

```
app.get("/user/:id", async (req, res, next) =>
{

  try {

    const        user        =        await
getUserById(req.params.id);

    res.json(user);

  } catch (error) {

    next(error); // Pass error to the Express
error handler

  }

});
```

2. Handling Unexpected Request Payloads

Sometimes, requests fail because the payload isn't formatted correctly. If your API expects JSON but receives plain text, it can cause cryptic errors.

To debug, always log incoming requests:

javascript

```javascript
app.use(express.json());


app.post("/submit", (req, res) => {

  console.log("Received    request    body:", req.body);

  res.send("Data received");
});
```

If `req.body` is `undefined`, the issue is likely missing middleware:

javascript

```javascript
app.use(express.json()); // Ensure this is included before your routes
```

3. Debugging Middleware Issues

Middleware runs sequentially, so if one piece of middleware doesn't call `next()`, it can block all subsequent routes.

Example: A Middleware That Blocks Requests

javascript

```javascript
app.use((req, res, next) => {

  console.log("Middleware executed");

  // Forgot to call next(), so requests never reach the route handler

});
```

The fix? Always call `next()` unless explicitly sending a response:

javascript

```javascript
app.use((req, res, next) => {

  console.log("Middleware executed");

  next();

});
```

Best Practices for Debugging Express.js Apps

Use meaningful log messages – Avoid generic `console.log("error")`. Instead, log error details:

javascript

```
console.error(`Error       fetching       user:
${error.message}`);
```

- **Keep track of API call sequences** – When debugging complex requests, log the order in which functions execute.

- **Use environment variables** – Avoid hardcoding sensitive data in your code. Use `.env` files instead.

- **Break down problems into smaller parts** – If a large function isn't working, isolate specific parts to identify the issue.

- **Leverage Express's built-in error handling** – Use centralized error handlers instead of scattering `try...catch` blocks everywhere.

Chapter 3: Understanding HTTP, Middleware, and Routing

Introduction

Every time you load a webpage, check your email, or send a message through an app, you're interacting with the **Hypertext Transfer Protocol (HTTP)**. It's the backbone of the web, defining how data moves between clients (browsers, mobile apps) and servers. If you're building web applications with Express.js, understanding HTTP is non-negotiable.

But handling HTTP requests in Express isn't just about setting up routes. To build flexible and scalable applications, you need **middleware**—a powerful concept that lets you control request flow, process data, and handle errors efficiently.

In this chapter, we'll break down HTTP requests and responses, explore how middleware functions work in Express.js, and walk through creating API routes that handle different request methods like **GET, POST, PUT, and DELETE**. By the end, you'll not only know how routing works but also how to structure it for real-world applications.

3.1 Basics of HTTP Requests and Responses

Picture this: You open your favorite e-commerce website, browse through the products, add an item to your cart, and complete your purchase. Behind the scenes, a series of HTTP requests are being exchanged between your browser and the website's server. Every click, search, or form submission triggers a request, and the server responds with the relevant data.

As an Express.js developer, understanding **how HTTP works** is essential because every interaction in a web application revolves around requests and responses. If you don't grasp the fundamentals, debugging API issues, handling user data, or even designing scalable endpoints can quickly become frustrating.

This section will break down HTTP's core concepts, including **requests, responses, headers, status codes, and methods**. Instead of just definitions, we'll explore **real-world use cases** so you can start thinking like a backend developer.

Understanding HTTP Requests

An **HTTP request** is how a client (browser, mobile app, or another server) asks a web server for data. A request typically consists of:

1. **A Method** – Defines the action to be performed (GET, POST, PUT, DELETE, etc.).

2. **A URL (Uniform Resource Locator)** – Specifies where the request is going (e.g., `/products`).

3. **Headers** – Carry metadata like authentication tokens and content types.

4. **A Body (for some requests)** – Contains data, usually in JSON format, for POST and PUT

requests.

Example: A Simple HTTP Request

Let's say you open your browser and type:

arduino

```
https://example.com/products?category=laptops
```

Behind the scenes, your browser sends this request:

makefile

```
GET /products?category=laptops HTTP/1.1

Host: example.com

User-Agent: Mozilla/5.0
```

- GET is the HTTP method, requesting product data.

- /products?category=laptops is the endpoint with a **query parameter** (category=laptops).

- The **Host** header specifies the server domain.

- The **User-Agent** header identifies the client (browser).

Now, let's handle this request in Express.js.

Handling HTTP Requests in Express.js

Express makes it easy to receive and process HTTP requests. Here's how you handle a simple **GET request** in an Express application:

javascript

```javascript
const express = require("express");

const app = express();

app.get("/products", (req, res) => {

  console.log(req.query);  // Extract query parameters

  res.json({ message: "Here are the products", query: req.query });

});

app.listen(3000, () => console.log("Server running on port 3000"));
```

If a user visits http://localhost:3000/products?category=laptops, Express extracts the query parameter:

json

```json
{

  "message": "Here are the products",

  "query": { "category": "laptops" }
```

```
}
```

Path Parameters vs. Query Parameters

- **Query Parameters** (e.g., `?category=laptops`)
  are used for filtering or optional data.

- **Path Parameters** are part of the URL and used
  for identifying specific resources.

Example: Using Path Parameters

javascript

```javascript
app.get("/products/:id", (req, res) => {

  res.json({ productId: req.params.id });

});
```

A request to `/products/42` will return:

json

```json
{

  "productId": "42"

}
```

Understanding when to use **query parameters vs.
path parameters** will help you design cleaner and
more predictable APIs.

Understanding HTTP Responses

Status Code	Meaning	Example Scenario
200 OK	Request was successful	Fetching a product list
201 Created	Resource was created	A new user signed up
400 Bad Request	Client error (e.g., missing data)	User submits an empty form
401 Unauthorized	Authentication required	Accessing a protected route without a token
403 Forbidden	User lacks permissions	Trying to delete another user's account

404 Not Found	Requested resource does not exist	Fetching a product that doesn't exist
500 Internal Server Error	Unexpected server failure	Database connection issue

When a server processes a request, it sends back a **response**. A response consists of:

1. **A Status Code** – Indicates success, failure, or other results.

2. **Headers** – Contain metadata about the response.

3. **A Body** – The actual data, often in JSON format.

Common HTTP Status Codes

Sending Responses in Express.js

javascript

```javascript
app.get("/status", (req, res) => {

  res.status(200).json({ message: "Everything is working fine" });

});
```

For error handling:

javascript

```javascript
app.get("/error", (req, res) => {

  res.status(500).json({  error:   "Something
went wrong" });

});
```

Headers in HTTP Requests and Responses

Headers provide additional information about the request or response.

Common Request Headers

- **Authorization** – Used for authentication (Bearer token123).

- **Content-Type** – Specifies the type of data being sent (application/json).

- **User-Agent** – Identifies the client making the request.

Common Response Headers

- **Content-Type** – Tells the client the format of the response (application/json).

- **Cache-Control** – Defines caching policies.

- **Access-Control-Allow-Origin** – Manages cross-origin requests (CORS).

Example: Sending Custom Headers in Express.js

javascript

```javascript
app.get("/custom-header", (req, res) => {

  res.set("X-Custom-Header", "This is a custom value");

  res.json({ message: "Custom header added" });

});
```

On the client side, the response will include:

vbnet

```vbnet
X-Custom-Header: This is a custom value
```

Understanding headers helps when working with **authentication, security, and performance optimizations**.

Hands-on Exercise: Building a Simple API Endpoint

Let's create a basic Express API that:

- Accepts a **GET request** with a query parameter.

- Responds with JSON data.

- Returns proper HTTP status codes.

Implementation

javascript

```javascript
const express = require("express");
const app = express();


app.get("/search", (req, res) => {
  const query = req.query.q;
  if (!query) {
    return res.status(400).json({ error: "Query parameter 'q' is required" });
  }
  res.json({ message: `You searched for: ${query}` });
```

```
});

app.listen(3000,  ()  =>  console.log("Server
running on port 3000"));
```

Testing the API

1. Visit:
   `http://localhost:3000/search?q=Express.j`
   `s`

   - **Response:** { "message": "You searched
     for: Express.js" }

2. Visit: `http://localhost:3000/search`

   - **Response:** { "error": "Query
     parameter 'q' is required" } (400
     Bad Request)

This small exercise reinforces how to handle requests,
validate input, and return appropriate responses.

3.2 What is Middleware? Understanding How It Works in Express.js

Imagine you're building a web application, and every
incoming request needs to be **logged,
authenticated, parsed, and secured** before it
reaches your main route handlers. Without an efficient

way to manage this process, you'd end up duplicating code across multiple routes, leading to a maintenance nightmare.

This is where **middleware** comes in. Middleware functions in Express.js allow you to **intercept, modify, and process requests and responses** before they reach their final destination. Whether you're adding authentication, handling errors, or serving static files, middleware acts as a flexible and powerful **pipeline** that ensures your application runs smoothly.

In this chapter, we'll break down middleware into simple, practical concepts. We'll look at how middleware works, why it's essential, and how you can use it effectively to **streamline request handling, improve security, and structure your application efficiently**.

What is Middleware?

Middleware is simply a **function** that sits between an incoming request and the final route handler. It can **inspect, modify, or terminate** a request before passing it along.

Basic Structure of Middleware in Express.js

Every middleware function has access to three important objects:

- req (Request) – Contains request data like headers, query parameters, and the request body.

- res (Response) – Used to send responses back to the client.

- next – A function that passes control to the next middleware in the stack.

Here's a **basic middleware function** that logs request details:

javascript

```javascript
const express = require("express");

const app = express();


const logger = (req, res, next) => {

  console.log(`[${new Date().toISOString()}] ${req.method} ${req.url}`);

  next(); // Pass control to the next middleware or route handler

};


app.use(logger);


app.get("/", (req, res) => {
```

```
  res.send("Hello, World!");

});


app.listen(3000, () => console.log("Server
running on port 3000"));
```

Breaking it Down:

1. **The `logger` function** runs before any route
   handler.

2. It logs the HTTP method and URL of each
   request.

3. It calls `next()` to ensure the request **continues**
   to the next middleware or route.

Without `next()`, the request would **hang
indefinitely**, because it wouldn't know where to go
next.

Types of Middleware in Express.js

Middleware in Express can be categorized into several
types, each serving a different purpose.

1. Application-Level Middleware

This type of middleware applies to **every request** in the application. It's useful for global concerns like **logging, authentication, and request parsing**.

Example:

javascript

```
app.use((req, res, next) => {

  console.log("Global middleware executed");

  next();

});
```

2. Route-Specific Middleware

If you only need middleware for certain routes, you can apply it selectively.

Example:

javascript

```
const checkAuth = (req, res, next) => {

  const token = req.headers.authorization;

  if (!token) {

    return  res.status(401).json({  error:
"Unauthorized" });
```

```javascript
  }

  next();

};

app.get("/protected", checkAuth, (req, res) =>
{

  res.send("This is a protected route");

});
```

3. Built-in Middleware

Express provides **built-in middleware functions** to handle common tasks.

- `express.json()` – Parses JSON request bodies.

- `express.urlencoded()` – Parses URL-encoded form data.

- `express.static()` – Serves static files.

Example:

javascript

```javascript
app.use(express.json());   //  Enables   JSON
parsing

app.use(express.urlencoded({  extended:  true
})); // Enables form data parsing
```

4. Third-Party Middleware

You can extend Express functionality using third-party middleware libraries.

- `cors` – Handles Cross-Origin Resource Sharing.

- `morgan` – Logs HTTP requests.

- `helmet` – Adds security headers.

Example:

javascript

```
const cors = require("cors");

app.use(cors());
```

Real-World Use Cases for Middleware

Middleware isn't just a concept—it's essential in real-world applications. Let's explore some practical use cases.

1. Logging Requests for Debugging

When debugging, you often need to know what requests are coming in. Instead of adding `console.log()` everywhere, you can use middleware.

javascript

```javascript
const morgan = require("morgan");

app.use(morgan("dev"));
```

2. Handling Authentication

Instead of manually checking authentication in every route, middleware centralizes it.

javascript

```javascript
const authenticate = (req, res, next) => {

  if (!req.headers.authorization) {

    return res.status(403).json({ error: "No
token provided" });

  }

  next();
};



app.use("/api", authenticate);
```

Now, all routes under /api require authentication.

3. Handling Errors Gracefully

Without proper error handling, users may see **ugly, unhelpful error messages**. Middleware can handle errors in a clean way.

javascript

```
app.use((err, req, res, next) => {

  console.error(err.stack);

  res.status(500).json({ error: "Something went wrong!" });

});
```

4. Serving Static Files

If your app needs to serve images, CSS, or JavaScript files, `express.static()` makes it easy.

javascript

```
app.use(express.static("public"));
```

Now, `public/index.html` is available at `http://localhost:3000/index.html`.

Hands-on Exercise: Custom Middleware for Request Timing

Let's create a middleware function that measures how long each request takes.

Implementation

javascript

```javascript
const requestTime = (req, res, next) => {

  req.requestTime = Date.now();

  next();

};



app.use(requestTime);



app.get("/", (req, res) => {

  const   timeTaken   =   Date.now()   -
req.requestTime;

  res.json({   message:   "Hello,   World!",
responseTime: `${timeTaken}ms` });

});
```

What Happens?

1. The middleware stores the **current timestamp** in `req.requestTime`.

2. The route handler calculates the time taken.

3. The response includes how long the request took.

This is useful for **performance monitoring** and **API response time tracking**.

3.3 Creating Your First Express.js Route

Introduction

You've just set up an Express.js application. The server is running, but right now, it doesn't do much. What if you wanted to display a homepage, provide an API endpoint, or handle user input? That's where **routes** come in.

Routes are the foundation of any web application. They determine how your server responds when a user visits a particular URL. Whether you're building a simple webpage, a RESTful API, or a complex web service, understanding how routing works in Express.js is **essential**.

In this chapter, we'll start from the basics—creating your first route, understanding HTTP methods, and exploring real-world routing patterns. By the end, you'll have a solid grasp of how to structure your Express.js routes effectively.

Understanding Routes in Express.js

A **route** in Express.js is simply a way to define how the server should respond to a specific request. Each route consists of:

1. **A URL path** – The address where the route is accessible (e.g., `/`, `/users`, `/api/products`).

2. **An HTTP method** – Defines the type of request (`GET`, `POST`, `PUT`, `DELETE`).

3. **A callback function** – Handles the request and sends back a response.

Basic Route Structure

Every route in Express follows this basic format:

javascript

```
app.METHOD(PATH, HANDLER);
```

- `app` – The Express application instance.

- `METHOD` – The HTTP method (`get`, `post`, `put`, `delete`).

- `PATH` – The URL where the route is accessible.

- `HANDLER` – A function that runs when the route is requested.

Now, let's see it in action.

Creating Your First Route

Let's start by setting up a simple Express.js server and defining a basic route.

Step 1: Initialize an Express App

First, create a new JavaScript file (server.js) and set up an Express server:

javascript

```javascript
const express = require("express");

const app = express();

const PORT = 3000;

app.listen(PORT, () => {

  console.log(`Server is running on port ${PORT}`);

});
```

Run this file with:

bash

```bash
node server.js
```

At this point, the server is running but doesn't do anything useful yet. Let's fix that.

Step 2: Define a Basic Route

Now, let's create a simple route that responds with "Hello, World!" when users visit the homepage (/).

javascript

```javascript
app.get("/", (req, res) => {

  res.send("Hello, World!");

});
```

Restart the server, open a browser, and go to http://localhost:3000/. You should see:

```
Hello, World!
```

Understanding What Happens

1. A GET request is made to /.

2. Express matches it to our app.get("/") route.

3. The callback function runs and sends "Hello, World!" as the response.

Working with Different HTTP Methods

In real applications, different actions require different HTTP methods:

- GET – Retrieve data (e.g., fetch user details).

- POST – Send new data (e.g., create a new user).

- PUT – Update existing data (e.g., edit a profile).

- DELETE – Remove data (e.g., delete a record).

Example: Defining Multiple Routes

javascript

```javascript
app.get("/about", (req, res) => {
  res.send("About Page");
});


app.post("/submit", (req, res) => {
  res.send("Form Submitted");
});


app.put("/update", (req, res) => {
  res.send("Data Updated");
});
```

```
app.delete("/delete", (req, res) => {
  res.send("Data Deleted");
});
```

Testing the Routes

- Open `http://localhost:3000/about` in your browser – you'll see `"About Page"`.

- Use Postman or cURL to test `POST`, `PUT`, and `DELETE` requests.

Example cURL command for testing a `POST` request:

bash

```
curl -X POST http://localhost:3000/submit
```

Handling Dynamic Routes with Parameters

Sometimes, you need routes that **accept dynamic values**. For example, if you're building a user profile page, you might have a route like `/users/:id`.

Example: Route Parameters

javascript

```javascript
app.get("/users/:id", (req, res) => {

  res.send(`User ID: ${req.params.id}`);

});
```

Now, if a user visits http://localhost:3000/users/123, they'll see:

sql

```sql
User ID: 123
```

Using Multiple Route Parameters

javascript

```javascript
app.get("/posts/:postId/comments/:commentId",
(req, res) => {

  res.json({

    postId: req.params.postId,

    commentId: req.params.commentId

  });

});
```

80

A request to `http://localhost:3000/posts/42/comments/99` returns:

json

```json
{
  "postId": "42",
  "commentId": "99"
}
```

Using Query Parameters for Optional Data

Sometimes, you want to **filter or modify** data using query parameters. Query parameters are added to the URL using ? and &.

Example: Handling Query Parameters

javascript

```javascript
app.get("/search", (req, res) => {
  const query = req.query.q || "No search term provided";
  res.send(`You searched for: ${query}`);
});
```

Now, visiting `http://localhost:3000/search?q=express` returns:

81

yaml

You searched for: express

Best Practices for Defining Routes

1. **Organize routes logically** – Keep related routes together.

2. **Use meaningful route names** – `/users/:id` is better than `/u/:id`.

3. **Validate inputs** – Always check `req.params` and `req.query` to prevent errors.

4. **Use middleware for reusable logic** – For authentication, logging, etc.

5. **Group routes using Express Router** – We'll cover this in a later chapter.

Hands-On Exercise: Building a Simple API Route

Let's create an API route that returns a **list of products** in JSON format.

javascript

```
app.get("/api/products", (req, res) => {
  const products = [
    { id: 1, name: "Laptop", price: 1000 },
    { id: 2, name: "Phone", price: 500 }
  ];
  res.json(products);
});
```

Try It Out

1. Restart your server.

2. Visit http://localhost:3000/api/products.

3. You'll see a JSON response like this:

json

```
[
  { "id": 1, "name": "Laptop", "price": 1000 },
  { "id": 2, "name": "Phone", "price": 500 }
]
```

This is the **foundation of RESTful APIs**, and we'll dive deeper into it in later chapters.

3.4 Handling GET, POST, PUT, DELETE Requests

Building a web application is more than just serving static content. As soon as you start handling user interactions—whether it's retrieving data, submitting forms, updating records, or deleting entries—you'll need to work with different HTTP methods.

Imagine you're developing a **simple task management system**. A user wants to:

- View their list of tasks

- Add a new task

- Update an existing task

- Remove a task they no longer need

Each of these actions corresponds to an HTTP method:

- **GET** for retrieving tasks

- **POST** for creating new tasks

- **PUT** for updating tasks

- **DELETE** for removing tasks

In this chapter, we'll explore how to handle these HTTP methods in Express.js, diving into real-world use cases and best practices along the way.

Understanding HTTP Methods in Express.js

HTTP methods define the type of action a request is performing. While there are many HTTP methods, Express.js applications primarily use these four:

- **GET** – Retrieve data (e.g., fetching a list of users)
- **POST** – Send new data (e.g., adding a new product)
- **PUT** – Modify existing data (e.g., updating user information)
- **DELETE** – Remove data (e.g., deleting a record from the database)

Mapping HTTP Methods to CRUD Operations

In most applications, these methods align with **CRUD (Create, Read, Update, Delete)** operations:

HTTP Method	Action	Example Use Case
GET	Read	Fetching a list of products
POST	Create	Adding a new user
PUT	Update	Editing a blog post

DELETE	Delete	Removing a user account

Now, let's dive into each method and see how to implement them in Express.js.

Handling GET Requests

A **GET request** is used to fetch data. Whether you're retrieving a list of users or displaying a blog post, GET is the method to use.

Example: Retrieving All Tasks

Let's create a basic route that returns a list of tasks.

javascript

```javascript
app.get("/tasks", (req, res) => {

  const tasks = [

    { id: 1, title: "Buy groceries", completed: false },

    { id: 2, title: "Read a book", completed: true }

  ];

  res.json(tasks);

});
```

Testing the Route

Run your Express server and visit `http://localhost:3000/tasks` in your browser. You should see:

json

```
[

  { "id": 1, "title": "Buy groceries",
"completed": false },

  { "id": 2, "title": "Read a book",
"completed": true }

]
```

Handling Dynamic Routes

Sometimes, you need to fetch a specific item by ID. You can use **route parameters** to achieve this.

javascript

```
app.get("/tasks/:id", (req, res) => {

  const taskId = req.params.id;

  res.send(`Fetching task with ID:
${taskId}`);

});
```

Visiting `http://localhost:3000/tasks/3` would return:

87

csharp

```
Fetching task with ID: 3
```

Handling POST Requests

A **POST request** is used to send new data to the server, such as creating a new user or adding an item to a database.

Example: Adding a New Task

Before handling a POST request, we need to **enable request body parsing** using Express's built-in middleware:

javascript

```
app.use(express.json());
```

Now, let's define a route to accept a new task:

javascript

```
app.post("/tasks", (req, res) => {

  const newTask = req.body;

  newTask.id = Math.floor(Math.random() * 1000); // Simulate an ID

  res.status(201).json(newTask);
```

```
});
```

Testing the Route with cURL

Since POST requests don't work in a browser, you can use Postman or cURL:

bash

```bash
curl -X POST http://localhost:3000/tasks -H
"Content-Type: application/json" -d '{"title":
"Write Express.js guide", "completed": false}'
```

Expected response:

json

```json
{

  "title": "Write Express.js guide",

  "completed": false,

  "id": 745

}
```

Common Mistakes with POST Requests

- **Forgetting** express.json() **middleware** –
  Without this, req.body will be undefined.

- **Not validating input data** – Always check if required fields exist before saving to a database.

Handling PUT Requests

A **PUT request** is used to update an existing resource. This is useful for modifying user details, changing a blog post, or updating task status.

Example: Updating a Task

javascript

```javascript
app.put("/tasks/:id", (req, res) => {

  const taskId = req.params.id;

  const updatedTask = req.body;


  res.json({    message:    `Task    ${taskId}
updated`, updatedTask });

});
```

Testing with cURL

bash

```bash
curl -X PUT http://localhost:3000/tasks/1 -H
"Content-Type: application/json" -d '{"title":
"Buy groceries", "completed": true}'
```

Expected response:

json

```json
{
  "message": "Task 1 updated",
  "updatedTask": {
    "title": "Buy groceries",
    "completed": true
  }
}
```

PUT vs PATCH

- PUT replaces the entire resource.

- PATCH updates only the provided fields.

For example, if a task has title and completed fields, sending a PUT request with only title will remove the completed field. Use PATCH when updating partial data.

Handling DELETE Requests

A **DELETE request** is used to remove a resource from the server, such as deleting a user account or removing a task.

Example: Deleting a Task

javascript

```javascript
app.delete("/tasks/:id", (req, res) => {

  const taskId = req.params.id;

  res.json({ message: `Task ${taskId} deleted`
});

});
```

Testing with cURL

bash

```bash
curl -X DELETE http://localhost:3000/tasks/2
```

Expected response:

json

```json
{

  "message": "Task 2 deleted"

}
```

Common Mistakes with DELETE Requests

- **Not checking if the resource exists** – Always verify before deleting.

- **Using GET instead of DELETE** – Ensure you're using the correct method.

Best Practices for Handling HTTP Methods in Express.js

1. **Use meaningful status codes** – 201 Created for POST, 404 Not Found when a resource doesn't exist.

2. **Validate request data** – Ensure the incoming data has required fields before processing.

3. **Avoid exposing sensitive actions in GET requests** – Use POST, PUT, or DELETE instead.

4. **Use middleware for authentication and validation** – Protect endpoints from unauthorized access.

5. **Handle errors gracefully** – Return meaningful error messages rather than generic responses.

PART 2: BUILDING EXPRESS.JS APPLICATIONS

Chapter 4: Working with Templating Engines and Static Files

Introduction

You're building a modern web application—perhaps a blog, an online store, or a dashboard. You need a way to display **styled** and **interactive** pages that can adapt to user data. Simply sending raw HTML from your Express server isn't enough.

This is where **static files** (CSS, JavaScript, images) and **templating engines** come into play. They help structure your application's frontend efficiently, making it easier to manage layouts, reuse components, and dynamically inject content.

- **Static files** let you serve stylesheets, scripts, and images to the browser.

- **Templating engines** allow you to generate dynamic HTML using variables and logic.

In this chapter, we'll explore both approaches. First, we'll see how to **serve static files** in Express.js. Then, we'll compare popular **templating engines** like **EJS, Handlebars, and Pug**, before diving into rendering dynamic content.

4.1 Serving Static Files (CSS, JavaScript, Images)

Imagine you're building a modern web application. You've set up your Express.js backend, created API routes, and connected your database. But when you visit your site, it looks plain—unstyled, without interactive behavior, and missing essential images.

Every dynamic web application needs **static assets**— CSS for styling, JavaScript for interactivity, and images for visual elements. Without them, your site is nothing more than a collection of raw HTML pages.

In traditional web servers like Apache or Nginx, serving static files is a built-in feature. But Express, being a minimal framework, doesn't expose static files by default. You have to configure it manually. Fortunately, Express provides a simple and efficient way to serve static assets using **express.static()**.

In this section, we'll explore how to serve static files, structure them properly, and avoid common pitfalls that can cause broken styles, missing images, or JavaScript errors.

Understanding Static Files in Express.js

A **static file** is any asset that doesn't change dynamically on the server. This includes:

- **CSS files** – Styles for your HTML pages

- **JavaScript files** – Client-side scripts for interactivity

- **Images** – Logos, icons, and other visuals

- **Fonts** – Custom fonts used in the application

- **Other assets** – PDFs, videos, and other static resources

Since these files do not require server-side processing, they should be delivered as efficiently as possible. Express's **express.static()** middleware helps us achieve this.

Serving Static Files with Express

Basic Setup

Let's assume you have the following project structure:

bash

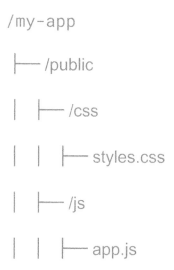

```
/my-app

├── /public

│   ├── /css

│   │   ├── styles.css

│   ├── /js

│   │   ├── app.js
```

```
|   ├── /images

|   |   ├── logo.png

├── server.js
```

The `public` directory will contain all static files. In your `server.js` file, set up Express and enable static file serving:

javascript

```javascript
const express = require("express");

const app = express();

const path = require("path");


// Serve static files from the "public" directory

app.use(express.static(path.join(__dirname, "public")));


app.get("/", (req, res) => {

  res.sendFile(path.join(__dirname, "public", "index.html"));
```

```
});
```

```
app.listen(3000, () => {

  console.log("Server        running        on
http://localhost:3000");

});
```

Now, when you visit `http://localhost:3000`, the `index.html` file inside `public` will load. Any CSS, JavaScript, or images referenced in `index.html` will be automatically served.

Accessing Static Files

By default, `express.static()` makes files available at their relative paths. If you have a CSS file located at `/public/css/styles.css`, you can include it in your HTML like this:

html

```
<link rel="stylesheet"
href="/css/styles.css">
```

Similarly, you can include JavaScript files:

html

```
<script src="/js/app.js"></script>
```

And display images:

html

```html
<img src="/images/logo.png" alt="Logo">
```

There's no need to specify `/public` in the URL—Express automatically serves files from this directory.

Using a Virtual Path Prefix

Sometimes, you might want to serve static files under a specific path instead of directly exposing them. You can achieve this by specifying a virtual prefix:

javascript

```javascript
app.use("/static",
express.static(path.join(__dirname,
"public")));
```

Now, all static files must be accessed with `/static` as a prefix:

html

```html
<link                    rel="stylesheet"
href="/static/css/styles.css">

<script src="/static/js/app.js"></script>

<img             src="/static/images/logo.png"
alt="Logo">
```

This approach can be useful for better **URL structuring** or **avoiding conflicts** with other routes.

Best Practices for Structuring Static Files

For maintainability and scalability, organize your static files properly:

- **Keep CSS, JavaScript, and images in separate folders** (`/css`, `/js`, `/images`)

- **Use a logical naming convention** (`app.js` instead of `script.js`)

- **Minify and bundle assets** to improve performance

- **Version static files** to prevent caching issues (e.g., `app-v1.js`)

Handling Common Pitfalls

1. Static Files Not Loading

If your CSS or JavaScript files are not loading, check:

- That you have included `express.static()` in your server setup

- The correct file paths in your HTML

- The browser's developer console for 404 errors

You can verify that your files are being served correctly by manually visiting `http://localhost:3000/css/styles.css` in your browser. If the file loads, Express is serving it correctly.

2. Browser Caching Issues

Browsers cache static files aggressively, which can cause issues when updating styles or scripts. To force the browser to load the latest version, append a query string:

html

```
<link                          rel="stylesheet"
href="/css/styles.css?v=1.1">
```

For a more automated approach, you can use **content hashing** in production environments.

3. Security Considerations

- **Do not expose sensitive files** – Make sure your static directory only contains public assets.

- **Use helmet middleware** – The helmet package adds security headers to prevent attacks.

- **Limit file access** – If you need more control over which files are served, consider using route-based file serving instead of `express.static()`.

Hands-On Project: Adding Static Assets to an Express App

Now that you understand how to serve static files, let's apply it by adding CSS, JavaScript, and an image to an Express-powered webpage.

1. Create a Simple HTML File

Inside the `public` folder, create an `index.html` file:

html

```
<!DOCTYPE html>

<html lang="en">

<head>

    <meta charset="UTF-8">

    <meta                          name="viewport"
content="width=device-width,           initial-
scale=1.0">

    <title>My Express App</title>

    <link                       rel="stylesheet"
href="/css/styles.css">
```

```html
</head>

<body>

    <h1>Welcome to My Express App</h1>

    <p>This is a simple webpage served by
Express.js.</p>

    <button        onclick="showAlert()">Click
Me</button>

    <script src="/js/app.js"></script>

</body>

</html>
```

2. Add CSS for Styling

Inside `public/css/styles.css`:

css

```css
body {

    font-family: Arial, sans-serif;

    background-color: #f4f4f4;

    text-align: center;

    margin: 50px;

}
```

```css
button {

    padding: 10px 20px;

    font-size: 16px;

}
```

3. Add JavaScript for Interactivity

Inside `public/js/app.js`:

javascript

```javascript
function showAlert() {

    alert("Hello! Static files are working in
Express.");

}
```

Now, start your Express server and visit `http://localhost:3000`. Your static files should load, making the webpage interactive and styled.

4.2 Using Templating Engines: EJS vs. Handlebars vs. Pug

You're building a dynamic web application with Express.js. Your server is handling routes, fetching data from a database, and sending responses to users.

But something feels inefficient—every time you need to display dynamic content, you're manually concatenating HTML strings in your route handlers.

It might start like this:

javascript

```javascript
app.get("/profile", (req, res) => {

  const user = { name: "Alice", age: 25 };

  res.send(`<h1>Welcome,
${user.name}</h1><p>Age: ${user.age}</p>`);

});
```

For small applications, this might seem fine. But as your project grows, this approach quickly becomes unmanageable. Writing HTML inside JavaScript leads to messy, unreadable code, and maintaining templates becomes a nightmare.

This is where **templating engines** come in. Templating engines allow you to separate HTML structure from JavaScript logic, making your code cleaner, more maintainable, and easier to scale.

In this chapter, we'll explore three popular templating engines for Express.js—**EJS, Handlebars, and Pug**—comparing their syntax, features, and best use cases. By the end, you'll have a solid understanding of how to integrate templating into your Express applications and choose the right engine for your needs.

What is a Templating Engine?

A **templating engine** is a tool that helps you generate dynamic HTML on the server side before sending it to the browser. Instead of writing raw HTML inside JavaScript, you use a template file with placeholders that get replaced with actual data when the page is rendered.

Templating engines bring several advantages:

- **Separation of concerns** – Keep HTML and JavaScript logic separate.

- **Reusability** – Use layouts and partial templates to avoid repetition.

- **Readability** – Cleaner, more structured HTML.

- **Maintainability** – Easier to update and scale applications.

Express supports multiple templating engines, but the most commonly used ones are **EJS, Handlebars, and Pug**. Let's dive into each.

EJS (Embedded JavaScript Templates)

EJS is one of the simplest and most popular templating engines for Express. It looks almost like regular HTML but allows you to embed JavaScript using `<%= %>` and `<% %>` syntax.

Installing and Setting Up EJS

First, install EJS:

bash

```
npm install ejs
```

Then, configure Express to use EJS as the templating engine:

javascript

```javascript
const express = require("express");

const app = express();

app.set("view engine", "ejs"); // Set EJS as
the view engine

app.use(express.static("public")); // Serve
static assets

app.get("/", (req, res) => {

  const user = { name: "Alice", age: 25 };

  res.render("index", { user });

});

app.listen(3000, () => console.log("Server
running on port 3000"));
```

EJS Syntax and Usage

Create a `views/index.ejs` file:

html

```
<!DOCTYPE html>

<html lang="en">

<head>

    <meta charset="UTF-8">

    <meta                          name="viewport"
content="width=device-width,           initial-
scale=1.0">

    <title>Welcome</title>

</head>

<body>

    <h1>Welcome, <%= user.name %></h1>

    <p>Age: <%= user.age %></p>

</body>

</html>
```

EJS provides:

- `<%= %>` – Outputs and escapes values

- `<%- %>` – Outputs without escaping

- `<% %>` – Executes JavaScript logic

For example, looping through an array:

html

```
<ul>
  <% users.forEach(user => { %>
    <li><%= user.name %></li>
  <% }) %>
</ul>
```

Pros and Cons of EJS

Familiar syntax (HTML-based)
Supports JavaScript directly
Easy to integrate into existing projects

No built-in layouts or partials (requires additional setup)
Can get cluttered with too much logic in templates

Handlebars (HBS)

Handlebars is another popular templating engine that enforces **logic-less templates**, making it more structured than EJS. It uses {{ }} syntax for placeholders.

110

Installing and Setting Up Handlebars

bash

```bash
npm install express-handlebars
```

Set it up in Express:

javascript

```javascript
const express = require("express");
const { engine } = require("express-handlebars");
const app = express();


app.engine("hbs", engine({ extname: ".hbs" }));
app.set("view engine", "hbs");


app.get("/", (req, res) => {
  const user = { name: "Alice", age: 25 };
  res.render("index", { user });
});
```

```
app.listen(3000, () => console.log("Server
running on port 3000"));
```

Handlebars Syntax and Usage

Create a `views/index.hbs` file:

html

```html
<!DOCTYPE html>

<html lang="en">

<head>

    <meta charset="UTF-8">

    <meta                              name="viewport"
content="width=device-width,                 initial-
scale=1.0">

    <title>Welcome</title>

</head>

<body>

    <h1>Welcome, {{user.name}}</h1>

    <p>Age: {{user.age}}</p>

</body>

</html>
```

Handlebars supports:

- **Conditionals**:

html

```
{{#if user.admin}}
  <p>Welcome, Admin!</p>
{{else}}
  <p>Welcome, User!</p>
{{/if}}
```

- **Loops**:

html

```
<ul>
  {{#each users}}
    <li>{{this.name}}</li>
  {{/each}}
</ul>
```

Pros and Cons of Handlebars

Enforces cleaner, logic-less templates
Supports partials and layouts out of the box
Widely used in large applications

Less flexible than EJS (no inline JavaScript)
More setup required for advanced features

Pug (formerly Jade)

Pug is a templating engine with a unique indentation-based syntax. It removes the need for traditional HTML tags, making templates more concise.

Installing and Setting Up Pug

bash

```
npm install pug
```

Set it up in Express:

javascript

```
const express = require("express");

const app = express();

app.set("view engine", "pug");

app.get("/", (req, res) => {

  const user = { name: "Alice", age: 25 };

  res.render("index", { user });
```

```
});
```

```
app.listen(3000, () => console.log("Server
running on port 3000"));
```

Pug Syntax and Usage

Create a `views/index.pug` file:

pug

```
doctype html
html(lang="en")
  head
    title Welcome
  body
    h1 Welcome, #{user.name}
    p Age: #{user.age}
```

Pros and Cons of Pug

Concise, clean syntax
Built-in conditionals and loops
Supports layouts and mixins

Steeper learning curve
Can be harder to debug for beginners

Which One Should You Use?

Feature	EJS	Handlebars	Pug
HTML-like syntax	Yes	Yes	NO
Supports JavaScript	Yes	NO	Yes
Built-in layouts	No	Yes	Yes
Readability	Yes	Yes	No (Indentation-based)
Performance	⚡ Fast	⚡ Fast	⚡ Fast

If you want **flexibility and minimal setup**, go with **EJS**.

If you prefer **structured, logic-less templates**, use **Handlebars**.

If you like **clean, minimal syntax**, try **Pug**.

4.3 Rendering Dynamic Content in Express.js

Imagine you're building a news website where headlines, articles, and images change daily. Hardcoding HTML files isn't an option—you need a way to dynamically generate pages based on real-time data. This is a common challenge in web development: how do you efficiently send dynamic content to the frontend while keeping your code clean and maintainable?

In Express.js, rendering dynamic content is a fundamental task. Whether you're displaying user profiles, product listings, or blog posts, you'll need a way to inject data into your views. This is where **templating engines** come in, allowing you to merge JavaScript logic with HTML structure.

In this chapter, we'll explore how Express.js handles dynamic content rendering, covering best practices, debugging insights, and real-world use cases. By the end, you'll be comfortable setting up and using templates to generate dynamic pages on the fly.

Why Do We Need Dynamic Rendering?

Static HTML pages work well for simple sites, but they don't scale for applications that require real-time updates or user-specific content. Consider an e-commerce site:

- A homepage needs to display the latest products.

- A user dashboard should show personalized recommendations.

- A search results page must update based on user queries.

Manually creating an HTML file for each variation would be inefficient. Instead, we use **server-side rendering (SSR)** to generate HTML dynamically before sending it to the browser.

Express.js makes this process seamless by integrating with templating engines like **EJS, Handlebars, and Pug**, allowing developers to populate views with data efficiently.

Setting Up Dynamic Rendering in Express.js

Before rendering dynamic content, ensure your Express application is configured to use a templating engine. For this example, we'll use **EJS** since it closely resembles HTML and integrates well with JavaScript.

Step 1: Install and Configure EJS

Install EJS via npm:

bash

```
npm install ejs
```

Set it up in Express:

javascript

```javascript
const express = require("express");

const app = express();

app.set("view engine", "ejs"); // Set EJS as
the view engine

app.use(express.static("public")); // Serve
static assets

app.listen(3000, () => console.log("Server
running on port 3000"));
```

Rendering Data from Express Routes

With EJS set up, let's create a dynamic page that
displays a list of users.

Step 2: Create a Route with Dynamic Data

javascript

```javascript
app.get("/users", (req, res) => {

  const users = [

    { name: "Alice", age: 25 },

    { name: "Bob", age: 30 },
```

```
    { name: "Charlie", age: 22 },
  ];


  res.render("users", { users });
});
```

Here, we're passing an array of user objects to the users.ejs template.

Step 3: Create the EJS Template

Create a views/users.ejs file:

html

```
<!DOCTYPE html>

<html lang="en">

<head>

    <meta charset="UTF-8">

    <meta                          name="viewport"
content="width=device-width,              initial-
scale=1.0">

    <title>User List</title>

</head>

<body>
```

```html
    <h1>User List</h1>

    <ul>

        <% users.forEach(user => { %>

            <li><%= user.name %> - Age: <%=
user.age %></li>

        <% }) %>

    </ul>

</body>

</html>
```

This template iterates over the `users` array and dynamically inserts names and ages into the HTML.

Handling Conditional Rendering

Sometimes, you need to display content conditionally. For example, showing a "No users found" message when the list is empty.

Modify the `users.ejs` template:

html

```html
<% if (users.length > 0) { %>

    <ul>

        <% users.forEach(user => { %>
```

```
        <li><%= user.name %> - Age: <%=
user.age %></li>

        <% }) %>

    </ul>

<% } else { %>

    <p>No users found.</p>

<% } %>
```

This ensures your UI remains clean even when no data is available.

Passing URL Parameters for Personalized Content

Let's say we want to display a personalized message for a specific user based on their ID.

Step 4: Define a Route with a Parameter

javascript

```
app.get("/user/:name", (req, res) => {

  const users = {

    Alice: { age: 25, role: "Admin" },

    Bob: { age: 30, role: "User" },

    Charlie: { age: 22, role: "Guest" },
```

```
  };

  const user = users[req.params.name];

  if (user) {
    res.render("profile",        {        name:
req.params.name, user });
  } else {
    res.status(404).send("User not found");
  }
});
```

Step 5: Create the Profile Template

Create views/profile.ejs:

html

```
<!DOCTYPE html>
<html lang="en">
<head>
    <meta charset="UTF-8">
```

```
    <meta                    name="viewport"
content="width=device-width,          initial-
scale=1.0">

    <title>Profile</title>

</head>

<body>

    <h1>Profile of <%= name %></h1>

    <p>Age: <%= user.age %></p>

    <p>Role: <%= user.role %></p>

</body>

</html>
```

Now, visiting `/user/Alice` dynamically renders Alice's profile, while `/user/Bob` shows Bob's information.

Fetching Data from a Database

Hardcoding data inside routes isn't ideal. In real-world applications, dynamic content often comes from a database. Here's how you can integrate MongoDB with Mongoose to render data from a collection.

Step 6: Connect to MongoDB

First, install Mongoose:

bash

```bash
npm install mongoose
```

Set up a connection in your Express app:

javascript

```javascript
const mongoose = require("mongoose");


mongoose.connect("mongodb://localhost:27017/myapp", {
  useNewUrlParser: true,
  useUnifiedTopology: true,
});
const User = mongoose.model("User", new mongoose.Schema({ name: String, age: Number }));


app.get("/db-users", async (req, res) => {
  const users = await User.find();
  res.render("users", { users });
});
```

This retrieves all users from the database and renders them in the `users.ejs` template.

Debugging Common Issues

While working with dynamic rendering, you might encounter some common issues:

1. **Template Not Found**

   - Ensure the template file is inside the `views` folder.

   - Check the file extension (`.ejs`, `.hbs`, `.pug`).

2. **Undefined Data in the Template**

   - Verify that you're passing the correct object in `res.render()`.

   - Log `req.params` or `req.body` to debug missing values.

3. **Syntax Errors in Templates**

   - EJS: Ensure proper opening and closing `<% %>` tags.

   - Handlebars: Check for missing `{{}}`.

   - Pug: Maintain proper indentation.

Chapter 5: Building RESTful APIs with Express.js

APIs are the backbone of modern web applications. Whether you're building a social media platform, an e-commerce store, or a weather app, you'll need a way for the frontend to communicate with the backend. This is where RESTful APIs come in.

If you're developing a task management app. Users need to create, update, delete, and retrieve tasks. You could manually write different pages for each action, but that wouldn't scale. Instead, you build an API that handles these operations efficiently, allowing any client—whether a web app, mobile app, or third-party service—to interact with your data.

Express.js simplifies API development, providing a lightweight yet powerful framework for building scalable RESTful services. In this chapter, you'll learn how RESTful APIs work, how to design and implement them using Express, and best practices for structuring your API for maintainability and performance.

5.1 What are RESTful APIs?

Imagine you're building a mobile app for a to-do list. Users need to add, update, delete, and retrieve their tasks. The app's frontend (what users see) needs a way to talk to the backend (where data is stored). You could hardcode everything into a single application, but that wouldn't scale. Instead, you create a **RESTful API**—a structured way for different parts of an application to communicate over the web.

APIs (Application Programming Interfaces) are the backbone of modern software development, connecting web apps, mobile apps, and even IoT devices. Whether you're fetching weather data, integrating payment gateways, or interacting with a database, APIs power the exchange of data behind the scenes. RESTful APIs, in particular, have become the standard due to their simplicity, scalability, and ease of use.

In this section, we'll explore what RESTful APIs are, how they work, and why they are the preferred choice for building modern web services.

Understanding RESTful APIs

A **RESTful API** is a web service that follows the principles of **REST (Representational State Transfer)**. It enables applications to communicate over HTTP using standard methods like GET, POST, PUT, and DELETE. Each request is stateless, meaning the server doesn't remember past interactions, making REST APIs highly scalable and efficient.

Key Characteristics of RESTful APIs

1. **Stateless** – Each API request must contain all the necessary information. The server doesn't store user sessions.

2. **Resource-Based** – Everything is treated as a resource (e.g., users, products, orders), identified by a unique URL.

3. **Uniform Interface** – The API follows consistent naming and request patterns.

4. **Client-Server Separation** – The frontend and backend interact only through API calls, making them independent.

5. **Cacheable** – Responses can be cached to improve performance and reduce server load.

How RESTful APIs Work

At its core, a REST API revolves around **resources**—entities like users, posts, or products. Each resource has a **URL endpoint**, and different HTTP methods determine how clients interact with it.

Consider a simple task management API:

HTTP Method	Endpoint	Action
GET	/tasks	Retrieve all tasks
GET	/tasks/:id	Retrieve a specific task
POST	/tasks	Create a new task
PUT	/tasks/:id	Update an existing task
DELETE	/tasks/:id	Delete a task

A GET /tasks request returns all tasks, while a DELETE /tasks/5 request removes the task with ID 5. By structuring APIs this way, they remain predictable and easy to work with.

Real-World Example: A Task Manager API

Let's break this down with a practical example. Imagine you're building a task management app where users can create and manage their tasks.

A **client** (such as a web or mobile app) sends a request to retrieve tasks:

http

```
GET /tasks HTTP/1.1

Host: api.example.com
```

The **server** responds with a JSON array of tasks:

json

```
[

    { "id": 1, "title": "Buy groceries",
"completed": false },

    { "id": 2, "title": "Read a book",
"completed": true }
```

```
]
```

If a user adds a new task, the client sends:

http

```
POST /tasks HTTP/1.1

Content-Type: application/json


{

    "title": "Write blog post",

    "completed": false

}
```

The server processes the request and responds with the newly created task:

json

```
{

    "id": 3,

    "title": "Write blog post",

    "completed": false
```

}

This structured approach makes it easy to extend the API, integrate with other services, and scale as the application grows.

Why RESTful APIs Matter

1. Simplicity and Scalability

RESTful APIs use standard HTTP methods, making them easy to implement and scale. Since requests are stateless, servers don't have to track session data, allowing them to handle more requests efficiently.

2. Flexibility and Integration

A well-designed REST API can be used across multiple platforms. A single API can serve web applications, mobile apps, and even third-party integrations without modification.

3. Decoupling Frontend and Backend

REST enforces a clear separation between frontend and backend, making it easier for teams to work independently. The frontend only needs to know the API endpoints, while backend developers focus on logic and data handling.

4. Standardization

Since REST follows a common structure, developers can quickly understand and use APIs without extensive documentation. Standardized error responses and status codes improve consistency across different projects.

Common Pitfalls and Best Practices

1. Poorly Designed Endpoints

A common mistake is using non-descriptive or inconsistent URLs. For example:

Bad:

bash

```
/getTasks

/createTask

/updateTask
```

Good:

bash

```
/tasks

/tasks/:id
```

Follow RESTful conventions for a cleaner and more predictable API.

2. Ignoring HTTP Status Codes

Proper status codes provide clarity when debugging API calls.

Status Code	Meaning
200 OK	Successful request
201 Created	Resource successfully created
400 Bad Request	Invalid client request
401 Unauthorized	Authentication required
404 Not Found	Requested resource not found
500 Internal Server Error	Server-side issue

3. Not Validating User Input

APIs must validate incoming data to prevent errors and security issues. If a client sends an empty task title, the server should reject it:

json

```json
{

    "error": "Task title is required"

}
```

Using a validation library like Joi ensures data integrity.

javascript

```javascript
const Joi = require("joi");

const schema = Joi.object({

    title: Joi.string().min(3).required(),

    completed: Joi.boolean()

});
```

4. Overcomplicating API Responses

Keep responses simple and consistent. Clients should receive structured, readable data rather than deeply nested objects.

5.2 Designing and Implementing a Simple API

Picture this: You're building a new web application, maybe a to-do list, a blog, or an e-commerce store. At some point, your frontend needs to fetch data from a backend service. Maybe it needs to display a list of tasks, fetch user profiles, or process payments. This is where an API comes in.

APIs allow different parts of an application—or even entirely separate applications—to communicate with each other. And in the world of web development, **RESTful APIs** are the standard. But understanding the theory behind REST is one thing; actually building a working API is another.

That's what we're going to do in this chapter. We'll **design and implement a simple API using Express.js**, covering everything from structuring routes to handling requests and responses. By the end, you'll have built a fully functional API that follows best practices and is ready to be expanded for real-world applications.

Let's get started.

Setting Up an Express.js Project

Before we dive into coding, let's make sure you have everything set up.

Prerequisites

To follow along, ensure you have:

- **Node.js and npm installed** (Check with `node -v` and `npm -v`)

- **Basic understanding of JavaScript and Express.js**

- **A code editor (VS Code recommended)**

Project Setup

First, create a new project folder and initialize a Node.js project:

sh

```sh
mkdir express-api && cd express-api

npm init -y
```

Next, install **Express.js**:

sh

```sh
npm install express
```

Now, create a file named `server.js` and open it in your editor.

Building a Simple API

For this example, let's create a **task management API** that allows users to manage their tasks.

1. Setting Up an Express Server

In `server.js`, start by requiring Express and creating an instance of an Express app:

JavaScript (server.js)

javascript

```javascript
const express = require("express");
```

```
const app = express();

app.use(express.json());    //   Middleware   to
parse JSON request bodies


const PORT = process.env.PORT || 3000;

app.listen(PORT,    ()   =>   console.log(`Server
running on port ${PORT}`));
```

Run the server:

sh

```
node server.js
```

If everything is working, your terminal should show:

arduino

```
Server running on port 3000
```

2. Designing API Endpoints

For our task manager API, we'll define these
endpoints:

HTTP Method	Endpoint	Action
GET	/tasks	Retrieve all tasks

GET	/tasks/:id	Retrieve a single task
POST	/tasks	Create a new task
PUT	/tasks/:id	Update a task
DELETE	/tasks/:id	Delete a task

3. Implementing CRUD Operations

We'll store tasks in an array for simplicity.

Retrieving All Tasks

Let's start by defining a route to get all tasks:

javascript

```javascript
const tasks = [

    { id: 1, title: "Buy groceries", completed: false },

    { id: 2, title: "Read a book", completed: true }

];


app.get("/tasks", (req, res) => {

    res.json(tasks);

});
```

When a client makes a GET /tasks request, the server responds with a list of tasks.

Retrieving a Single Task

To fetch a specific task by ID:

javascript

```javascript
app.get("/tasks/:id", (req, res) => {

    const task = tasks.find(t => t.id === parseInt(req.params.id));

    if (!task) return res.status(404).json({ error: "Task not found" });

    res.json(task);

});
```

If the task exists, we return it; otherwise, we send a **404 Not Found** error.

Creating a New Task

Now, let's allow users to add a task using a POST request:

javascript

```
app.post("/tasks", (req, res) => {

    const { title, completed } = req.body;

    if (!title) return res.status(400).json({
error: "Title is required" });


    const newTask = {

        id: tasks.length + 1,

        title,

        completed: completed || false

    };

    tasks.push(newTask);

    res.status(201).json(newTask);

});
```

- We extract the title and completed values
  from req.body.

- If the title is missing, we return a 400 Bad
  Request error.

- Otherwise, we create a new task, add it to the
  array, and return it with a **201 Created** status.

Updating a Task

To modify an existing task:

javascript

```
app.put("/tasks/:id", (req, res) => {

    const task = tasks.find(t => t.id ===
parseInt(req.params.id));

    if (!task) return res.status(404).json({
error: "Task not found" });


    const { title, completed } = req.body;

    if (title) task.title = title;

    if    (completed    !==    undefined)
task.completed = completed;


    res.json(task);

});
```

This route updates the task **only** if valid fields are
provided.

Deleting a Task

Finally, let's implement task deletion:

javascript

```javascript
app.delete("/tasks/:id", (req, res) => {

    const index = tasks.findIndex(t => t.id
=== parseInt(req.params.id));

    if      (index      ===      -1)      return
res.status(404).json({ error: "Task not found"
});



    tasks.splice(index, 1);

    res.json({   message:   "Task   deleted
successfully" });

});
```

Testing the API

You can test your API using **Postman** or **cURL**. Here's
how to send a POST request using cURL:

sh

```sh
curl -X POST http://localhost:3000/tasks -H
"Content-Type: application/json" -d '{"title":
"Write blog post", "completed": false}'
```

Common Mistakes and Best Practices

1. Proper Error Handling

Always return meaningful error messages and appropriate HTTP status codes.

Bad:

javascript

```javascript
if (!task) res.send("Error");
```

Good:

javascript

```javascript
if (!task) return res.status(404).json({
error: "Task not found" });
```

2. Using Middleware for JSON Parsing

Instead of manually parsing request bodies, always use `express.json()`.

javascript

```javascript
app.use(express.json());
```

3. Keeping Routes Modular

As your API grows, move routes into separate files instead of keeping everything in `server.js`.

5.3 Handling Query Parameters and Request Bodies

Imagine you're building an e-commerce API, and a frontend developer needs to retrieve a list of products. But they don't want every product—just the ones that are in stock and priced below $50. Similarly, when a customer places an order, the API needs to process and store order details, like product IDs, quantities, and customer information.

How do we handle these kinds of dynamic requests in Express.js?

This is where **query parameters and request bodies** come into play. Query parameters let users filter and customize requests, while request bodies allow clients to send structured data to the server— essential for creating, updating, and processing resources.

In this chapter, we'll break down both concepts, explore real-world use cases, and walk through practical implementations. By the end, you'll have a solid grasp of how to handle dynamic user input in your Express.js applications.

Understanding Query Parameters

What Are Query Parameters?

Query parameters are key-value pairs appended to the end of a URL, allowing clients to send additional information to the server. They're commonly used for:

- **Filtering data** (e.g., GET /products?category=electronics)

- **Sorting results** (e.g., GET /products?sort=price&order=asc)

- **Pagination** (e.g., GET /users?page=2&limit=10)

Extracting Query Parameters in Express

Express makes it easy to retrieve query parameters using req.query. Let's say we have a GET /products endpoint that supports filtering by category and price range.

JavaScript (server.js)

javascript

```
const express = require("express");

const app = express();
```

```javascript
const products = [

    { id: 1, name: "Laptop", category:
"electronics", price: 999 },

    { id: 2, name: "Headphones", category:
"electronics", price: 49 },

    { id: 3, name: "Chair", category:
"furniture", price: 150 }

];


app.get("/products", (req, res) => {

    let filteredProducts = [...products];


    if (req.query.category) {

        filteredProducts                    =
filteredProducts.filter(p  =>  p.category  ===
req.query.category);

    }


    if (req.query.maxPrice) {

        filteredProducts                    =
filteredProducts.filter(p   =>   p.price   <=
parseFloat(req.query.maxPrice));
```

```
    }


    res.json(filteredProducts);

});



const PORT = process.env.PORT || 3000;

app.listen(PORT, () => console.log(`Server
running on port ${PORT}`));
```

Testing Query Parameters

If you start your server and request:

bash

```
GET /products?category=electronics
```


The response will return only electronic products.

If you add a price filter:

bash

```
GET
/products?category=electronics&maxPrice=50
```

You'll get only the **Headphones**, since it's the only electronic item under $50.

Understanding Request Bodies

What Are Request Bodies?

While query parameters modify **what** data is retrieved, request bodies allow clients to **send** structured data—commonly used for:

- **Submitting forms** (e.g., user sign-ups, logins)

- **Creating new resources** (e.g., adding products, registering users)

- **Updating existing resources** (e.g., modifying account details)

In Express, request bodies are typically sent in **JSON format** using POST, PUT, or PATCH requests.

Handling JSON Request Bodies in Express

Before accessing request bodies, we need to enable express.json() middleware:

javascript

```
app.use(express.json());
```

Without this, Express won't automatically parse incoming JSON data.

Creating a New Resource Using Request Bodies

Let's say we want to allow users to add new products using a POST /products endpoint.

JavaScript (server.js)

javascript

```javascript
app.post("/products", (req, res) => {
    const { name, category, price } = req.body;


    if (!name || !category || price ===
undefined) {
        return res.status(400).json({ error:
"Name, category, and price are required" });
    }


    const newProduct = {
        id: products.length + 1,
        name,
        category,
        price: parseFloat(price)
    };
```

```
    products.push(newProduct);

    res.status(201).json(newProduct);
});
```

Testing Request Bodies

Using **cURL** or **Postman**, you can send a POST request
with a JSON body:

sh

```
curl -X POST http://localhost:3000/products \

    -H "Content-Type: application/json" \

    -d '{"name": "Table", "category":
"furniture", "price": 200}'
```

The response should return the newly added product.

Combining Query Parameters and Request Bodies

Now, let's consider a **real-world use case** where a
user can:

- **Fetch products with query parameters** (GET
  /products?category=furniture)

- **Add new products with a request body**
  (`POST /products`)

- **Update existing products using both URL parameters and a request body** (`PUT /products/:id`)

Updating a Product

To modify an existing product's details, we'll use the product ID as a **URL parameter** (`req.params.id`) and updated fields in the **request body** (`req.body`).

javascript

```javascript
app.put("/products/:id", (req, res) => {

    const product = products.find(p => p.id
=== parseInt(req.params.id));

    if           (!product)            return
res.status(404).json({ error: "Product not
found" });


    const { name, category, price } = req.body;


    if (name) product.name = name;

    if (category) product.category = category;
```

```
    if (price !== undefined) product.price =
parseFloat(price);


    res.json(product);
});
```

Testing the Update Route

You can send an update request:

sh

```
curl -X PUT http://localhost:3000/products/1 \
    -H "Content-Type: application/json" \
    -d '{"price": 899}'
```

Now, when you fetch products again, the price of the **Laptop** should be updated.

Common Mistakes and Best Practices

1. Always Validate User Input

Failing to validate request bodies can lead to **unexpected errors or security vulnerabilities**. Use a validation library like **Joi** or manually check required fields before processing data.

2. Use Default Values for Optional Parameters

If a query parameter isn't provided, set a default instead of returning an error.

Bad:

javascript

```
if (!req.query.limit) return
res.status(400).json({ error: "Limit is
required" });
```

Good:

javascript

```
const limit = req.query.limit ?
parseInt(req.query.limit) : 10;
```

3. Keep URLs RESTful and Meaningful

Instead of designing confusing or overly complex routes, stick to intuitive RESTful principles:

Bad:

bash

```
GET /fetchProducts?category=electronics
```

Good:

bash

```
GET /products?category=electronics
```

5.4 Best Practices for Structuring Express.js APIs

If you've ever worked on a growing Express.js project, you've likely experienced the slow creep of messy code. At first, a single `server.js` file with a few routes seems fine. But as the project scales—new features, multiple endpoints, authentication layers—the once-simple codebase turns into a tangled web of callbacks, repeated logic, and unclear folder structures.

Sound familiar?

This is a common challenge for developers building APIs with Express.js. Without a solid structure, your API becomes difficult to manage, debug, and extend. But by following best practices, you can build an API that is **scalable, maintainable, and easy to understand**.

In this chapter, we'll cover key strategies for structuring an Express.js API the right way. You'll learn how to organize files, separate concerns, handle errors effectively, and apply middleware efficiently. By the end, you'll have a framework for building well-structured APIs that can grow without turning into a maintenance nightmare.

1. Organizing the Project Structure

One of the biggest mistakes beginners make is keeping everything in a single file. While this works for simple experiments, real-world projects need **a clear structure**.

A Better Folder Structure

A common and effective way to structure an Express.js API is:

bash

```
/my-api

|— /src

|    |— /routes

|    |    |— products.routes.js

|    |    |— users.routes.js

|    |— /controllers

|    |    |— products.controller.js

|    |    |— users.controller.js
```

```
|    ├── /models
|    |   ├── product.model.js
|    |   ├── user.model.js
|    ├── /middlewares
|    |   ├── auth.middleware.js
|    |   ├── error.middleware.js
|    ├── /config
|    |   ├── db.config.js
|    |   ├── env.config.js
|    ├── app.js
|    ├── server.js
├── package.json
├── .env
├── README.md
```

Breaking It Down

- `routes/`: Defines API endpoints and connects them to controllers

- `controllers/`: Handles business logic, keeping route files clean

- `models/`: Defines data structures and interacts with the database

- `middlewares/`: Stores middleware functions for authentication, logging, etc.

- `config/`: Stores database configurations and environment variables

- `app.js`: Initializes Express and middleware

- `server.js`: Starts the server

By separating concerns, you make the API easier to manage, test, and scale.

2. Implementing the Controller-Service Pattern

Mixing route definitions with business logic makes code harder to maintain. Instead, use the **controller-service pattern**, which separates request handling from business logic.

Without Controllers (Bad Practice)

javascript

```javascript
app.get("/products", async (req, res) => {

    const products = await Product.find();

    res.json(products);

});
```

This works, but as complexity grows, route files get cluttered.

With Controllers (Better Approach)

routes/products.routes.js

javascript

```javascript
const express = require("express");

const router = express.Router();

const productController =
require("../controllers/products.controller")
;



router.get("/",
productController.getAllProducts);



module.exports = router;
```

controllers/products.controller.js

javascript

```javascript
const ProductService = require("../services/products.service");


exports.getAllProducts = async (req, res, next) => {
    try {
        const products = await ProductService.getAll();

        res.json(products);
    } catch (error) {
        next(error);
    }
};
```

services/products.service.js

javascript

```
const              Product              =
require("../models/product.model");


exports.getAll = async () => {

    return await Product.find();

};
```

Why This Matters

- Keeps route files clean

- Encourages reusability by separating business logic

- Makes unit testing easier

---

3. Middleware for Cleaner Code

Middleware functions help **avoid repeating code** across routes. Common use cases include:

- **Authentication & authorization**

- **Logging requests**

- **Error handling**

Example: Authentication Middleware

middlewares/auth.middleware.js

javascript

```javascript
const jwt = require("jsonwebtoken");


exports.authenticate = (req, res, next) => {
    const token = req.header("Authorization");

    if (!token) return res.status(401).json({
error: "Access denied" });


    try {
        const decoded = jwt.verify(token,
process.env.JWT_SECRET);

        req.user = decoded;

        next();
    } catch (err) {
        res.status(400).json({          error:
"Invalid token" });

    }
};
```


Then, use it in routes:

163

javascript

```javascript
const                authMiddleware                =
require("../middlewares/auth.middleware");


router.get("/profile",
authMiddleware.authenticate,
userController.getProfile);
```

Now, all requests to `/profile` require authentication, keeping our controller clean.

4. Proper Error Handling

Instead of cluttering every function with `try...catch`, use a centralized error-handling middleware.

Error Middleware

`middlewares/error.middleware.js`

javascript

```javascript
exports.errorHandler = (err, req, res, next)
=> {

    console.error(err.stack);
```

```javascript
  res.status(err.status    ||    500).json({
error: err.message || "Internal Server Error"
});

};
```

Using It in Express

javascript

```javascript
app.use(require("./middlewares/error.middlewa
re").errorHandler);
```

Now, whenever an error is thrown inside an async function, it gets handled automatically.

---

5. Using Environment Variables for Configuration

Hardcoding API keys, database URLs, or secrets in your code is a **security risk**. Instead, store them in a .env file and load them using dotenv.

Example .env File

ini

```ini
PORT=3000

MONGO_URI=mongodb://localhost:27017/mydb

JWT_SECRET=mysecretkey
```

Loading `.env` **in Express**

javascript

```javascript
require("dotenv").config();

const PORT = process.env.PORT || 3000;

app.listen(PORT, () => console.log(`Server running on port ${PORT}`));
```

This keeps secrets out of source control and makes configuration easy to change.

---

6. Versioning Your API

As your API evolves, breaking changes can disrupt existing clients. To avoid this, use **versioned endpoints**.

Example: API Versioning

Instead of:

bash

```bash
/users
```

Use:

bash

```
/api/v1/users
```

Then, in `server.js`:

javascript

```
app.use("/api/v1/users",
require("./routes/users.routes"));
```

This way, when a new version is released, old clients can continue using `/api/v1/`, while new clients adopt `/api/v2/`.

Chapter 6: Connecting Express.js with Databases (MongoDB & MySQL)

6.1 Introduction to Database Integration

Why Do We Need a Database?

Let's say you're building a simple note-taking app with Express.js. You start by storing notes in an array like this:

javascript

```
const notes = [

    { id: 1, title: "Learn Express.js",
content: "Start with routing and middleware"
},

    { id: 2, title: "Build a REST API",
content: "Implement CRUD operations" },

];
```

It works fine—until you restart the server. Suddenly, all the notes are gone. If multiple users need to store notes, things get even messier. How do you manage user-specific data? How do you scale beyond your local machine?

This is where databases come in. A database allows us to store, retrieve, and manage data **persistently and efficiently**, ensuring that information is available across multiple sessions and users.

Databases in Web Applications

In modern web applications, almost every feature involves some kind of data storage:

- **User authentication** – Storing user credentials and login sessions

- **E-commerce** – Managing products, orders, and customer data

- **Social media** – Handling user profiles, posts, likes, and comments

Without a proper database, these applications simply wouldn't function. Express.js, being a lightweight web framework, doesn't have a built-in database. But it gives us the flexibility to integrate with various databases, allowing us to choose the best solution based on our needs.

SQL vs. NoSQL: Choosing the Right Database for Your App

Before jumping into code, it's important to understand **two main types of databases**:

1. Relational Databases (SQL)

Relational databases, such as **MySQL, PostgreSQL, and MariaDB**, store data in **structured tables** with defined relationships. These databases use **Structured Query Language (SQL)** for operations.

Best suited for:
Applications requiring structured relationships (e.g., an e-commerce store where orders must be linked to customers)
Data consistency and complex queries

Example Table (Users in MySQL):

id	name	email
1	Alice	alice@email.com
2	Bob	bob@email.com

To get all users, you would use SQL:

sql

```
SELECT * FROM users;
```

2. NoSQL Databases (MongoDB, Firebase, etc.)

NoSQL databases store data in **documents, key-value pairs, or graphs** instead of structured tables. MongoDB, one of the most popular NoSQL databases, stores data in **JSON-like documents** rather than rows and columns.

Best suited for:

Applications requiring flexible schema (e.g., dynamic content where fields may change over time)
High scalability with large datasets

Example Document (User in MongoDB):

json

```json
{
    "_id": "60c72b2f5f1b2c001f4e5b0a",
    "name": "Alice",
    "email": "alice@email.com"
}
```

SQL vs. NoSQL: When to Choose What?

Feature	SQL (MySQL, PostgreSQL)	NoSQL (MongoDB)
Data Structure	Tables with relations	JSON-like documents
Schema	Fixed, structured	Flexible, dynamic
Scalability	Vertical scaling	Horizontal scaling
Query Language	SQL	NoSQL queries (JSON-based)
Best For	Financial apps, e-commerce	Social networks, real-time apps

Both databases have their strengths. If you're building a **finance or inventory system**, go with SQL. If you're building a **social media app**, NoSQL might be a better choice.

How Express.js Connects to a Database

Express.js itself doesn't include database connectivity out of the box, but it can integrate seamlessly with both SQL and NoSQL databases using **ORMs (Object-Relational Mappers)** and **database drivers**.

For MongoDB (NoSQL)

We use **Mongoose**, a popular ODM (Object-Document Mapper), to define data models and interact with MongoDB:

javascript

```javascript
const mongoose = require("mongoose");

mongoose.connect("mongodb://localhost:27017/express_db", {

    useNewUrlParser: true,

    useUnifiedTopology: true

})

.then(() => console.log("MongoDB connected"))

.catch(err => console.error("MongoDB connection error:", err));
```

172

For MySQL (SQL)

For MySQL, we use **Sequelize**, an ORM that simplifies SQL queries:

javascript

```javascript
const { Sequelize } = require("sequelize");

const sequelize = new Sequelize("express_db", "root", "password", {

    host: "localhost",

    dialect: "mysql"

});

sequelize.authenticate()

    .then(() => console.log("MySQL connected"))

    .catch(err => console.error("MySQL connection error:", err));
```

Both methods allow Express.js to communicate with a database, whether it's relational (MySQL) or document-based (MongoDB).

Common Challenges When Working with Databases in Express.js

1. Connection Issues

Databases can sometimes fail to connect due to incorrect credentials, network issues, or misconfigured environment variables. Always use **try-catch blocks** to handle errors gracefully.

Example for MongoDB:

javascript

```
try {

    await
mongoose.connect(process.env.MONGO_URI);

} catch (error) {

    console.error("Database      connection
failed:", error);

}
```

2. Handling Large Data Sets

Fetching too much data at once can slow down your API. Use **pagination** to improve performance.

174

Example for MongoDB:

javascript

```
const users = await
User.find().limit(10).skip(20); // Get 10
users, skipping the first 20
```

3. Preventing SQL Injection & NoSQL Injection

When accepting user input, always **sanitize queries** to prevent attacks.

For MySQL:

javascript

```
const user = await sequelize.query("SELECT *
FROM users WHERE email = ?", {

    replacements: [req.body.email],

});
```

For MongoDB (using Mongoose):

javascript

```
const user = await User.findOne({ email:
req.body.email }); // Avoid raw JSON queries
```

Security should always be a priority when working with databases in Express.js.

6.2 Setting Up MongoDB with Mongoose

Why Mongoose?

Let's imagine you're building a to-do list app with Express.js. You need to store tasks persistently, so you decide to use MongoDB, a NoSQL database that handles JSON-like documents. But working directly with MongoDB can feel clunky—queries can be verbose, and data validation becomes a headache.

This is where **Mongoose** comes in. It acts as a bridge between your Express.js app and MongoDB, simplifying interactions by:

- **Defining schemas** to structure your data

- **Providing validation** to ensure data integrity

- **Making queries more readable** with built-in methods

With Mongoose, working with MongoDB feels more like working with objects in JavaScript. Instead of dealing with raw database queries, you interact with **models**, making data management cleaner and more intuitive.

Installing MongoDB and Mongoose

176

Before we dive into Mongoose, you need to set up MongoDB on your system.

1. Install MongoDB

If you haven't installed MongoDB yet, download it from the official website and follow the installation steps for your operating system.

To check if MongoDB is running, use:

sh

```
mongod --version
```

Once installed, start MongoDB using:

sh

```
mongod
```

By default, MongoDB runs on mongodb://localhost:27017, meaning it's available locally on port **27017**.

2. Install Mongoose

In your Express.js project, install Mongoose via npm:

sh

```
npm install mongoose
```

Now that we have both MongoDB and Mongoose installed, let's integrate them into our Express.js app.

Connecting Express.js to MongoDB with Mongoose

1. Establishing a Connection

In your Express project, create a new file `database.js` inside a `config` folder to manage your database connection.

javascript

```javascript
const mongoose = require("mongoose");

const connectDB = async () => {
    try {
        await mongoose.connect("mongodb://localhost:27017/express_app", {
            useNewUrlParser: true,
            useUnifiedTopology: true
        });
        console.log("MongoDB connected successfully");
```

```javascript
    } catch (error) {

        console.error("MongoDB     connection
error:", error);

        process.exit(1);

    }

};



module.exports = connectDB;
```

2. Integrating the Connection into Express.js

Now, modify `server.js` to connect to MongoDB before
starting the Express server:

javascript

```javascript
const express = require("express");

const            connectDB            =
require("./config/database");



const app = express();



// Connect to MongoDB
```

```
connectDB();


app.use(express.json());


app.get("/", (req, res) => {
    res.send("MongoDB   is   connected   with
Express!");
});


const PORT = process.env.PORT || 5000;
app.listen(PORT, () => console.log(`Server
running on port ${PORT}`));
```

How It Works:

1. We import Mongoose and define an **async function** to connect to MongoDB.

2. The connection uses **try-catch** to handle errors gracefully.

3. If MongoDB fails to connect, we **exit the process** to avoid running a broken app.

4. We call `connectDB()` in `server.js` before starting the server.

At this point, your Express.js app should successfully connect to MongoDB. If everything is set up correctly, running:

sh

```
node server.js
```

Should output:

arduino

```
MongoDB connected successfully

Server running on port 5000
```

Defining a Mongoose Schema and Model

Now that Express.js is connected to MongoDB, let's define a **Mongoose schema** to store data.

1. Creating a Schema

Inside a `models` folder, create a new file called `Task.js`:

javascript

```javascript
const mongoose = require("mongoose");
const TaskSchema = new mongoose.Schema({
    title: {
        type: String,
        required: [true, "Title is required"],
        trim: true
    },
    completed: {
        type: Boolean,
        default: false
    },
    createdAt: {
        type: Date,
        default: Date.now
    }
});
module.exports = mongoose.model("Task", TaskSchema);
```

2. Understanding the Schema

- `title`: A **required string** that gets trimmed to remove unnecessary spaces.

- `completed`: A **boolean** that defaults to `false`.

- `createdAt`: A **date** field that automatically stores the creation time.

This schema ensures **data consistency**, preventing issues like missing or incorrectly formatted fields.

CRUD Operations with Mongoose

Now, let's create routes to interact with the database.

1. Creating a Task (POST Request)

Modify `server.js` to include task management routes:

javascript

```javascript
const Task = require("./models/Task");

app.post("/tasks", async (req, res) => {

    try {

        const task = new Task(req.body);

        await task.save();

        res.status(201).json(task);
```

```javascript
    } catch (error) {

        res.status(400).json({                error:
error.message });

    }

});
```

How It Works:

- The user sends a **POST request** with task data.

- A new Task object is created and saved to MongoDB.

- If successful, we return the saved task with a **201 status**.

- If there's an error (e.g., missing title), we return a **400 status** with the error message.

2. Retrieving Tasks (GET Request)

javascript

```javascript
app.get("/tasks", async (req, res) => {

    try {

        const tasks = await Task.find();

        res.json(tasks);
```

```javascript
    } catch (error) {

        res.status(500).json({ error: "Server
error" });

    }

});
```

3. Updating a Task (PUT Request)

javascript

```javascript
app.put("/tasks/:id", async (req, res) => {

    try {

        const task = await
Task.findByIdAndUpdate(req.params.id,
req.body, { new: true });

        if (!task) return
res.status(404).json({ error: "Task not found"
});

        res.json(task);

    } catch (error) {

        res.status(400).json({ error:
error.message });

    }
```

```
});
```

4. Deleting a Task (DELETE Request)

javascript

```javascript
app.delete("/tasks/:id", async (req, res) => {
    try {
        const task = await
Task.findByIdAndDelete(req.params.id);

        if (!task) return
res.status(404).json({ error: "Task not found"
});

        res.json({ message: "Task deleted
successfully" });

    } catch (error) {
        res.status(500).json({ error: "Server
error" });

    }
});
```

Common Issues and Debugging Tips

1. MongoDB Connection Fails

- Ensure MongoDB is running (mongod command).

o Check if the correct database URL is used.

2. **Validation Errors**

o Mongoose throws errors if required fields are missing. Always check error messages.

3. **Empty Responses**

o Ensure you're using `await` when fetching data.

6.3 Using MySQL with Sequelize ORM

Why Use Sequelize with MySQL?

When building a full-stack web application where users can sign up, manage their profiles, and track their activities. Your data needs **structure**, relationships (like users and their posts), and the ability to run complex queries efficiently. While MongoDB is great for flexibility, relational databases like **MySQL** excel when you need structured, **ACID-compliant** data handling.

But working directly with raw SQL queries can get tedious. Writing queries manually, handling connections, and managing transactions quickly becomes repetitive. This is where **Sequelize**, a popular ORM (Object-Relational Mapper) for Node.js, comes into play.

Sequelize provides:

- **A structured way to define models** (tables) with clear relationships

- **Query abstraction**, allowing us to interact with the database using JavaScript instead of raw SQL

- **Built-in validation and hooks**, making it easier to enforce data integrity

Instead of writing SQL queries manually, Sequelize lets you interact with the database in a more natural, JavaScript-friendly way.

Setting Up MySQL and Sequelize

Before diving into Sequelize, let's set up MySQL and ensure everything is ready to go.

1. Install MySQL

If you haven't installed MySQL yet, download it from the official MySQL website and follow the installation steps for your operating system.

Once installed, start the MySQL service and log in to the MySQL shell:

sh

```
mysql -u root -p
```

Enter your password when prompted. Then, create a new database for your Express app:

sql

```sql
CREATE DATABASE express_app;
```

2. Install Sequelize and MySQL2 Driver

Sequelize needs a MySQL driver to communicate with the database. Install both dependencies using npm:

sh

```sh
npm install sequelize mysql2
```

Now that MySQL and Sequelize are installed, let's connect them to our Express.js application.

Connecting Express.js to MySQL with Sequelize

Create a config folder in your project and add a new file called database.js:

javascript

```javascript
const { Sequelize } = require("sequelize");
```

```javascript
const sequelize = new Sequelize("express_app",
"root", "password", {

    host: "localhost",

    dialect: "mysql",

    logging: false

});

const connectDB = async () => {

    try {

        await sequelize.authenticate();

        console.log("MySQL           connected
successfully");

    } catch (error) {

        console.error("MySQL           connection
error:", error);

        process.exit(1);

    }

};


module.exports = { sequelize, connectDB };
```

Breaking It Down:

- We create a **Sequelize instance** using the MySQL database credentials.

- The `authenticate()` method checks if the connection is working.

- If the connection fails, the app exits with an error message.

Now, update `server.js` to connect to the database before starting the Express server:

javascript

```javascript
const express = require("express");

const { connectDB } = require("./config/database");


const app = express();


// Connect to MySQL

connectDB();


app.use(express.json());


app.get("/", (req, res) => {
```

```
    res.send("MySQL    is    connected    with
Express!");
});
```

```
const PORT = process.env.PORT || 5000;
app.listen(PORT,  ()  =>  console.log(`Server
running on port ${PORT}`));
```

Run the server:

sh

```
node server.js
```

If everything is set up correctly, you should see:

arduino

```
MySQL connected successfully
Server running on port 5000
```

Defining Models with Sequelize

Now that Express is connected to MySQL, let's define a Sequelize model. Models in Sequelize represent **database tables** and define how data is structured.

1. Creating a Model for Users

Inside a new `models` folder, create a file called `User.js`:

javascript

```
const { Sequelize, DataTypes } =
require("sequelize");

const { sequelize } =
require("../config/database");


const User = sequelize.define("User", {

    id: {

        type: DataTypes.INTEGER,

        autoIncrement: true,

        primaryKey: true

    },

    name: {

        type: DataTypes.STRING,
```

```
        allowNull: false
    },
    email: {
        type: DataTypes.STRING,
        allowNull: false,
        unique: true,
        validate: {
            isEmail: true
        }
    },
    password: {
        type: DataTypes.STRING,
        allowNull: false
    }
}, {
    timestamps: true
});

module.exports = User;
```

How It Works:

- The `define()` method maps JavaScript objects to MySQL tables.

- `DataTypes.STRING`, `DataTypes.INTEGER`, etc., define column types.

- `allowNull: false` ensures certain fields cannot be empty.

- `validate: { isEmail: true }` ensures only valid emails are stored.

2. Syncing the Model with MySQL

Before using the model, we need to sync it with the database. Modify `database.js`:

javascript

```javascript
const User = require("../models/User");


const syncDB = async () => {
    try {
        await sequelize.sync({ alter: true });
```

```
        console.log("Database          synced
successfully");

    } catch (error) {

        console.error("Error          syncing
database:", error);

    }

};



module.exports   =   {   sequelize,   connectDB,
syncDB };
```

Now, update `server.js` to sync the database:

javascript

```
const    {    connectDB,    syncDB    }    =
require("./config/database");



(async () => {

    await connectDB();

    await syncDB();

})();
```

Run the server again. You should see:

nginx

```
Database synced successfully
```

Now the Users table exists in MySQL.

CRUD Operations with Sequelize

1. Creating a User (POST Request)

Modify server.js to handle user management routes:

javascript

```javascript
const User = require("./models/User");

app.post("/users", async (req, res) => {
    try {
        const user = await User.create(req.body);
        res.status(201).json(user);
```

```javascript
    } catch (error) {

        res.status(400).json({            error:
error.message });

    }

});
```

2. Retrieving Users (GET Request)

javascript

```javascript
app.get("/users", async (req, res) => {

    try {

        const users = await User.findAll();

        res.json(users);

    } catch (error) {

        res.status(500).json({ error: "Server
error" });

    }

});
```

3. Updating a User (PUT Request)

javascript

```javascript
app.put("/users/:id", async (req, res) => {
```

```javascript
    try {

        const          user          =          await
User.findByPk(req.params.id);

        if              (!user)              return
res.status(404).json({ error: "User not found"
});


        await user.update(req.body);

        res.json(user);

    } catch (error) {

        res.status(400).json({          error:
error.message });

    }

});
```

4. Deleting a User (DELETE Request)

javascript

```javascript
app.delete("/users/:id", async (req, res) => {

    try {
```

```
        const      user      =           await
User.findByPk(req.params.id);

        if             (!user)            return
res.status(404).json({ error: "User not found"
});


        await user.destroy();

        res.json({ message: "User deleted
successfully" });

    } catch (error) {

        res.status(500).json({ error: "Server
error" });

    }

});
```

Common Issues and Debugging Tips

1. Database Connection Fails

- Ensure MySQL is running: `mysql -u root -p`

- Double-check credentials in `database.js`.

2. **Unique Constraint Errors**

   ○ Ensure email values are unique.

   ○ Handle errors properly in `.catch()`.

3. **Query Returns Null**

   ○ Always check if `findByPk()` or `findOne()` return `null` before accessing properties.

6.4 CRUD Operations in Express.js with Databases

Why CRUD Operations Matter

In almost every real-world web application, data is at the core. Whether you're building a social media platform, an e-commerce site, or a simple to-do list, you need a way to **create**, **read**, **update**, and **delete** data—better known as CRUD operations.

Without CRUD, your app would be static, unable to persist user input or reflect changes dynamically. Imagine a user signing up for an account, but their information disappears after they refresh the page. Or an admin trying to update product details, only to realize there's no way to modify existing records. These basic operations make applications dynamic and functional.

In this chapter, we'll implement CRUD operations in an **Express.js application connected to a database**.

By the end, you'll have a clear understanding of how to manage data efficiently and securely.

Setting Up the Project

Before diving into CRUD operations, let's ensure we have an Express.js project set up with a database connection. If you haven't already, install Express and Sequelize (or your preferred ORM):

sh

```
npm install express sequelize mysql2 dotenv
```

- express: The web framework

- sequelize: The ORM for working with relational databases

- mysql2: The MySQL driver

- dotenv: For managing environment variables

Project Structure

To keep our project organized, we'll use the following structure:

bash

```
/express-crud-app

|— /config

|    ├— database.js

|— /models

|    ├— User.js

|— /routes

|    ├— userRoutes.js

|— server.js
```

- `/config/database.js`: Database connection
  setup

- `/models/User.js`: Defines our User model

- `/routes/userRoutes.js`: Handles CRUD routes

- `server.js`: Main entry point

Connecting Express to the Database

Inside `/config/database.js`, set up the connection to MySQL using Sequelize:

javascript

```javascript
const { Sequelize } = require("sequelize");

require("dotenv").config();


const sequelize = new Sequelize(process.env.DB_NAME,
process.env.DB_USER, process.env.DB_PASSWORD,
{

    host: process.env.DB_HOST,

    dialect: "mysql",

    logging: false,
});


const connectDB = async () => {

    try {

        await sequelize.authenticate();

        console.log("Connected to MySQL
database");
```

```
    } catch (error) {

        console.error("Database      connection
failed:", error);

        process.exit(1);

    }

};


module.exports = { sequelize, connectDB };
```

Environment Variables (.env file)

Create a .env file in the project root to store database credentials securely:

ini

```
DB_NAME=express_app

DB_USER=root

DB_PASSWORD=yourpassword

DB_HOST=localhost
```

Defining the User Model

Now, define a User model inside /models/User.js:

javascript

```javascript
const { DataTypes } = require("sequelize");
const { sequelize } = require("../config/database");

const User = sequelize.define("User", {
    id: {
        type: DataTypes.INTEGER,
        autoIncrement: true,
        primaryKey: true
    },
    name: {
        type: DataTypes.STRING,
        allowNull: false
    },
    email: {
        type: DataTypes.STRING,
```

```
        allowNull: false,

        unique: true,

        validate: {

            isEmail: true

        }

    },

    password: {

        type: DataTypes.STRING,

        allowNull: false

    }

}, {

    timestamps: true

});


module.exports = User;
```

Breaking It Down:

- Each **column** (name, email, password) is
  explicitly defined.

- allowNull: false ensures required fields are not empty.

- validate: { isEmail: true } enforces email format validation.

Creating CRUD Routes

Now, let's create API endpoints to perform CRUD operations in /routes/userRoutes.js.

1. Creating a New User (POST Request)

javascript

```
const express = require("express");

const User = require("../models/User");

const router = express.Router();

router.post("/", async (req, res) => {

    try {

        const user = await User.create(req.body);

        res.status(201).json(user);

    } catch (error) {

        res.status(400).json({ error: error.message });
```

```javascript
    }
});
```

```javascript
module.exports = router;
```

2. Retrieving All Users (GET Request)

javascript

```javascript
router.get("/", async (req, res) => {
    try {
        const users = await User.findAll();
        res.json(users);
    } catch (error) {
        res.status(500).json({ error: "Server
error" });
    }
});
```

3. Retrieving a Single User (GET Request by ID)

javascript

```javascript
router.get("/:id", async (req, res) => {

    try {

        const        user        =        await
User.findByPk(req.params.id);

        if            (!user)            return
res.status(404).json({ error: "User not found"
});


        res.json(user);

    } catch (error) {

        res.status(500).json({ error: "Server
error" });

    }

});
```

4. Updating a User (PUT Request)

javascript

```javascript
router.put("/:id", async (req, res) => {

    try {

        const        user        =        await
User.findByPk(req.params.id);
```

```javascript
    if              (!user)                 return
res.status(404).json({ error: "User not found"
});


       await user.update(req.body);

       res.json(user);

   } catch (error) {

       res.status(400).json({            error:
error.message });

   }

});
```

5. Deleting a User (DELETE Request)

javascript

```javascript
router.delete("/:id", async (req, res) => {

   try {

       const        user        =        await
User.findByPk(req.params.id);

       if              (!user)                 return
res.status(404).json({ error: "User not found"
});
```

```javascript
        await user.destroy();

        res.json({ message: "User deleted
successfully" });

    } catch (error) {

        res.status(500).json({ error: "Server
error" });

    }

});
```

Integrating Routes in `server.js`

Now, modify `server.js` to include these routes:

javascript

```javascript
const express = require("express");

const { connectDB } =
require("./config/database");

const userRoutes =
require("./routes/userRoutes");

const app = express();

app.use(express.json());
```

```
app.use("/users", userRoutes);


connectDB();

const PORT = process.env.PORT || 5000;

app.listen(PORT, () => console.log(`Server
running on port ${PORT}`));
```

Now, run the server:

sh

```
node server.js
```

Use **Postman** or **cURL** to test the API.

Common Issues and Debugging

1. **"ECONNREFUSED" Error on MySQL Connection**

   - Ensure MySQL is running: `mysql -u root -p`

   - Double-check credentials in `.env`.

2. **Sequelize Validation Errors**

- If `unique: true` is set for email, duplicate values will cause errors.

- Use proper error handling in `catch()` blocks.

3. **API Not Returning Data**

- Check if the `User.sync()` step is completed successfully.

PART 3: ADVANCED EXPRESS.JS CONCEPTS

Chapter 7: Authentication and Authorization

Why Authentication and Authorization Matter

When building an application where anyone can access user profiles, modify other people's data, or delete important records—without restriction. That would be a security nightmare.

Authentication and authorization form the backbone of secure web applications. Authentication ensures that users are **who they claim to be**, while authorization controls **what they can do** once authenticated.

In this chapter, we'll cover three critical aspects of securing an Express.js application:

1. **User Authentication with JWT (JSON Web Tokens)** – Securely verifying users.

2. **Securing Routes with Middleware** – Restricting access to protected resources.

3. **Implementing OAuth for Social Logins** – Allowing users to log in with Google and GitHub.

By the end of this chapter, you'll have a robust authentication system that balances security and usability.

7.1 User Authentication with JWT (JSON Web Tokens)

Why Authentication Matters

If you've built a simple web app where users can create and manage their notes. At first, everything works fine—anyone can add, edit, and delete notes. But soon, you realize a major problem: there's no way to distinguish one user from another. Any visitor can modify or delete someone else's notes. That's a security disaster waiting to happen.

This is where authentication comes in. Authentication ensures that users are **who they claim to be** before they can access protected resources. One of the most popular methods for handling authentication in modern web applications is **JWT (JSON Web Token)**.

In this section, we'll dive deep into:

- **How JWT works and why it's useful**

- **Setting up user authentication in an Express.js app**

- **Generating and verifying JWTs**

- **Common pitfalls and best practices**

By the end, you'll have a solid understanding of JWT authentication and how to implement it securely in your Express.js applications.

How JWT Works

JWT is a **stateless** authentication method, meaning the server does not store session information. Instead, a JWT is generated and sent to the client upon successful login. The client includes this token in subsequent requests, allowing the server to verify their identity.

A JWT consists of three parts, separated by dots (.):

1. **Header** – Specifies the token type (JWT) and the hashing algorithm used (e.g., HS256).

2. **Payload** – Contains user data (e.g., id, email) and additional claims (e.g., iat for issued time, exp for expiration).

3. **Signature** – A cryptographic signature that ensures the token hasn't been tampered with.

Here's what a decoded JWT might look like:

json

```
{

  "header": {

    "alg": "HS256",

    "typ": "JWT"

  },

  "payload": {
```

```
    "id": "12345",

    "email": "user@example.com",

    "iat": 1711926400,

    "exp": 1711930000

  },

  "signature": "abcdef1234567890"

}
```

This token is then sent with API requests in the **Authorization** header:

http

```
Authorization: Bearer <your_jwt_token_here>
```

The server verifies the token before granting access to protected resources.

Setting Up JWT Authentication in Express.js

Now, let's build a simple authentication system using JWT in an Express.js application.

1. Install Required Packages

First, install the necessary dependencies:

sh

```
npm install express jsonwebtoken bcryptjs
dotenv
```

- express – The web framework.

- jsonwebtoken – Used to generate and verify JWTs.

- bcryptjs – Securely hashes passwords.

- dotenv – Loads environment variables from a .env file.

Create a .env file and add:

ini

```
JWT_SECRET=your_secret_key

JWT_EXPIRATION=1h
```

2. Setting Up the Authentication Controller

Inside a new `/controllers/authController.js` file, define the authentication logic.

javascript

```javascript
const jwt = require("jsonwebtoken");

const bcrypt = require("bcryptjs");

const User = require("../models/User");


const generateToken = (user) => {

    return jwt.sign(

        { id: user.id, email: user.email },

        process.env.JWT_SECRET,

        {                           expiresIn:
process.env.JWT_EXPIRATION }

    );

};


// User Registration

exports.register = async (req, res) => {

    try {
```

```javascript
        const { name, email, password } =
req.body;


        // Hash the password before storing

        const   hashedPassword   =   await
bcrypt.hash(password, 10);

        const user = await User.create({ name,
email, password: hashedPassword });


        const token = generateToken(user);

        res.status(201).json({ user: { id:
user.id, email: user.email }, token });

    } catch (error) {

        res.status(400).json({           error:
error.message });

    }

};


// User Login

exports.login = async (req, res) => {

    try {
```

```
    const { email, password } = req.body;

    const user = await User.findOne({
where: { email } });



    if (!user || !(await
bcrypt.compare(password, user.password))) {

        return res.status(401).json({
error: "Invalid credentials" });

    }



    const token = generateToken(user);

    res.json({ user: { id: user.id, email:
user.email }, token });

  } catch (error) {

    res.status(500).json({ error: "Server
error" });

  }

};
```

- The `register` function hashes passwords before saving them to the database.

- The `login` function checks user credentials, and if valid, returns a JWT.

---

3. Creating Protected Routes

Now that users can log in and receive JWTs, we need to secure certain routes.

Create a middleware file: `/middleware/authMiddleware.js`

javascript

```
const jwt = require("jsonwebtoken");

const authenticate = (req, res, next) => {

    const token =
req.header("Authorization")?.split(" ")[1];

    if (!token) {

        return res.status(401).json({ error:
"Access denied. No token provided." });

    }

    try {

        const decoded = jwt.verify(token,
process.env.JWT_SECRET);

        req.user = decoded; // Attach user
data to request
```

```javascript
        next();

    } catch (error) {

        res.status(403).json({          error:
"Invalid token" });

    }

};
```

```javascript
module.exports = authenticate;
```

Apply this middleware to protected routes:

javascript

```javascript
const express = require("express");

const                authenticate                =
require("../middleware/authMiddleware");

const router = express.Router();


router.get("/profile",   authenticate,   async
(req, res) => {

    try {
```

```
        const         user         =         await
User.findByPk(req.user.id,  {  attributes:  {
exclude: ["password"] } });

        res.json(user);

    } catch (error) {

        res.status(500).json({ error: "Server
error" });

    }

});


module.exports = router;
```

Now, only users with a valid JWT can access /profile.

Common Mistakes and Best Practices

1. Never Store JWTs in Local Storage

Local storage is vulnerable to XSS attacks. Instead, store tokens in **HTTP-only cookies** for better security.

2. Use Short-Lived Tokens and Refresh Tokens

Tokens should have short expiration times (15m or 1h). Implement a refresh token system to issue new tokens without forcing frequent logins.

3. Validate and Sanitize User Inputs

Before saving user data, sanitize inputs to prevent SQL injection and other attacks.

4. Implement Role-Based Access Control (RBAC)

Add roles (e.g., admin, user) to the JWT payload and check permissions before granting access to specific routes.

7.2 Securing Routes with Middleware

Why Securing Routes Matters

Let's say you've built an API for a blogging platform. Users can create, edit, and delete their own blog posts. Everything works well—until you realize something alarming. Anyone who knows an API endpoint can delete any blog post, even if they don't own it.

This is a serious security flaw. If you don't properly **protect your routes**, you leave your application vulnerable to unauthorized access, data breaches, and abuse.

That's where **middleware** comes in. Middleware in Express.js allows you to create **reusable security layers** that protect sensitive routes and ensure users only access what they're allowed to.

In this chapter, we'll explore:

- **What middleware is and how it works**

- **How to use middleware for authentication and access control**

- **Common security vulnerabilities middleware can prevent**

- **Best practices for securing routes in Express.js**

By the end, you'll know how to implement middleware that **filters, validates, and protects your API routes**, ensuring only the right users have access.

What is Middleware in Express.js?

Middleware functions in Express.js are **functions that execute before the final route handler**. They have access to the request (req), response (res), and the next function, which determines whether to pass control to the next middleware in the stack.

Middleware is commonly used for:

- **Authentication** – Checking if a user is logged in

- **Authorization** – Verifying user roles and permissions

- **Request validation** – Ensuring incoming data is valid

- **Logging** – Tracking API requests and responses

- **Rate limiting** – Preventing excessive API calls

Here's a simple middleware example:

javascript

```javascript
const exampleMiddleware = (req, res, next) => {
    console.log(`Incoming request: ${req.method} ${req.url}`);
    next(); // Passes control to the next middleware or route handler
};

app.use(exampleMiddleware);
```

This middleware logs every request before allowing the request to continue.

Securing Routes with Authentication Middleware

In the previous section, we implemented **JWT-based authentication**. Now, we'll build a middleware function that ensures only authenticated users can access protected routes.

1. Creating an Authentication Middleware

Inside `/middleware/authMiddleware.js`, define the authentication function:

javascript

```javascript
const jwt = require("jsonwebtoken");


const authenticate = (req, res, next) => {

    const token = req.header("Authorization")?.split(" ")[1];


    if (!token) {

        return res.status(401).json({ error: "Access denied. No token provided." });

    }
```

```javascript
    try {

        const   decoded   =   jwt.verify(token,
process.env.JWT_SECRET);

        req.user  =  decoded;  //  Attach  user
data to the request object

        next();

    } catch (error) {

        res.status(403).json({            error:
"Invalid or expired token." });

    }

};


module.exports = authenticate;
```

2. Applying the Middleware to Secure Routes

Now, use the authenticate middleware in your route
file (routes/userRoutes.js):

javascript

```javascript
const express = require("express");
```

```javascript
const             authenticate              =
require("../middleware/authMiddleware");

const router = express.Router();


router.get("/profile",   authenticate,   async
(req, res) => {

    try {

        const        user        =        await
User.findByPk(req.user.id,  {  attributes:  {
exclude: ["password"] } });

        res.json(user);

    } catch (error) {

        res.status(500).json({ error: "Server
error" });

    }

});


module.exports = router;
```

Now, only users with a valid JWT token can access the
/profile route.

Implementing Role-Based Access Control (RBAC)

Authentication ensures that a user is logged in, but it doesn't check **what they're allowed to do**. A basic user shouldn't have the same permissions as an admin.

To solve this, let's build an **authorization middleware** that restricts access based on user roles.

1. Creating a Role-Based Middleware

Inside `/middleware/roleMiddleware.js`:

javascript

```
const authorize = (roles) => {

    return (req, res, next) => {

        if (!roles.includes(req.user.role)) {

            return        res.status(403).json({
error:    "Access    forbidden:    Insufficient
permissions." });

        }

        next();

    };

};

module.exports = authorize;
```

This function checks if the logged-in user has the required role before granting access.

2. Applying Role-Based Authorization to Routes

Modify `routes/adminRoutes.js` to restrict access to admins:

javascript

```javascript
const express = require("express");

const authenticate = require("../middleware/authMiddleware");

const authorize = require("../middleware/roleMiddleware");

const router = express.Router();



router.post("/delete-user/:id", authenticate,
authorize(["admin"]), async (req, res) => {

    try {

        const userId = req.params.id;

        await User.destroy({ where: { id:
userId } });

        res.json({ message: "User deleted
successfully." });
```

```
    } catch (error) {

        res.status(500).json({ error: "Server
error" });

    }

});



module.exports = router;
```

Now, only users with the `admin` role can delete other users.

Preventing Common Security Vulnerabilities

1. Protecting Against CSRF Attacks

Cross-Site Request Forgery (CSRF) attacks trick users into performing unwanted actions. To prevent this, **never use GET requests for actions like deleting data**. Instead, require POST, PUT, or DELETE methods and use CSRF tokens.

2. Avoiding Information Leaks in Error Messages

Never return detailed error messages that expose sensitive details. Instead of:

json

```json
{ "error": "Invalid token: Signature verification failed." }
```

Return a generic response:

json

```json
{ "error": "Invalid or expired token." }
```

This prevents attackers from gathering information about your security setup.

3. Implementing Rate Limiting

To prevent brute-force attacks, use rate limiting to **restrict the number of requests** from a single IP address.

Install express-rate-limit:

sh

```sh
npm install express-rate-limit
```

Create a rate limiter middleware:

javascript

```javascript
const rateLimit = require("express-rate-limit");
```

```javascript
const limiter = rateLimit({

    windowMs: 15 * 60 * 1000, // 15 minutes

    max: 100, // Limit each IP to 100 requests
per window

    message: { error: "Too many requests,
please try again later." }

});



module.exports = limiter;
```

Apply it globally in `server.js`:

javascript

```javascript
const express = require("express");

const               limiter               =
require("./middleware/rateLimitMiddleware");


const app = express();

app.use(limiter);
```

This helps protect your API from abuse and ensures fair usage.

7.3 Implementing OAuth for Social Logins (Google, GitHub)

Why Social Logins Matter

Imagine you're signing up for yet another web app. You see a long registration form asking for your name, email, and password. You sigh, consider whether you really need this account, and maybe—just maybe—decide it's not worth the effort.

Now, imagine an alternative: **"Sign in with Google"** or **"Sign in with GitHub"**. One click, a quick authorization step, and you're in. No passwords to remember, no forms to fill out.

That's the power of **OAuth-based social logins**. It improves the user experience, reduces friction, and enhances security by relying on trusted authentication providers.

In this chapter, we'll walk through:

- **What OAuth is and how it works**

- **How to implement Google and GitHub login in an Express.js app**

- **Handling authentication callbacks and storing user data**

- **Common pitfalls and best practices**

By the end, you'll have a fully working social login integration in your Express.js application.

Understanding OAuth: How It Works

OAuth 2.0 is an **authorization framework** that allows users to grant third-party applications access to their data **without sharing passwords**. Instead of logging in with a username and password, users authenticate through a provider like Google or GitHub.

The OAuth flow generally follows these steps:

1. **User clicks "Sign in with Google/GitHub"** – Your app redirects the user to the provider's login page.

2. **User logs in and grants permission** – The provider authenticates the user and asks if they want to share their profile details.

3. **Provider sends an authorization code** – If the user approves, the provider redirects back to your app with an authorization code.

4. **Your server exchanges the code for an access token** – Your app sends this code to the provider to get an access token, which allows you to request user details.

5. **User information is retrieved and authenticated** – Your app fetches the user's profile data and either logs them in or creates a new account.

Now, let's implement this flow in an Express.js app using **Passport.js**, a popular authentication middleware.

Setting Up Google OAuth in Express.js

1. Installing Dependencies

First, install the necessary packages:

sh

```
npm install passport passport-google-oauth20
express-session dotenv
```

- passport – Authentication middleware for Node.js

- passport-google-oauth20 – Google OAuth 2.0 strategy

- express-session – Stores user sessions

- `dotenv` – Loads environment variables

2. Configuring Google OAuth Credentials

Go to Google Cloud Console and:

1. Create a new project.

2. Enable the **Google+ API** (or "Google Identity" in newer versions).

3. Go to **Credentials → Create OAuth Client ID**.

4. Set the authorized redirect URI to `http://localhost:3000/auth/google/callback`.

Copy your **Client ID** and **Client Secret**, then add them to `.env`:

ini

```
GOOGLE_CLIENT_ID=your_google_client_id

GOOGLE_CLIENT_SECRET=your_google_client_secret

SESSION_SECRET=your_session_secret
```

3. Implementing Google OAuth with Passport.js

Initialize Passport and Sessions

In `server.js`, set up session management and Passport:

javascript

```javascript
const express = require("express");

const passport = require("passport");

const session = require("express-session");

require("dotenv").config();

require("./config/passport");    //    Import
Passport config

const app = express();

app.use(session({                           secret:
process.env.SESSION_SECRET,  resave:   false,
saveUninitialized: false }));

app.use(passport.initialize());

app.use(passport.session());


app.use("/auth",
require("./routes/authRoutes"));    //    OAuth
routes


app.listen(3000,  ()  =>  console.log("Server
running on http://localhost:3000"));
```

Configure Passport for Google OAuth

Create `config/passport.js`:

javascript

```javascript
const passport = require("passport");

const GoogleStrategy = require("passport-google-oauth20").Strategy;

passport.use(new GoogleStrategy({

    clientID: process.env.GOOGLE_CLIENT_ID,

    clientSecret: process.env.GOOGLE_CLIENT_SECRET,

    callbackURL: "/auth/google/callback"

}, (accessToken, refreshToken, profile, done) => {

    return done(null, profile);

}));



passport.serializeUser((user, done) => done(null, user));

passport.deserializeUser((obj, done) => done(null, obj));
```

Create Authentication Routes

Inside `routes/authRoutes.js`:

```javascript
const express = require("express");

const passport = require("passport");

const router = express.Router();

router.get("/google",
passport.authenticate("google",    {    scope:
["profile", "email"] }));


router.get("/google/callback",
passport.authenticate("google", {

    failureRedirect: "/login"

}), (req, res) => {

    res.redirect("/profile");

});


router.get("/logout", (req, res) => {

    req.logout((err) => {

        if (err) return next(err);

        res.redirect("/");

    });

});
```

```
module.exports = router;
```

Now, visiting `http://localhost:3000/auth/google` will initiate the login process.

Setting Up GitHub OAuth

1. Installing GitHub Strategy

sh

```
npm install passport-github2
```

2. Configuring GitHub OAuth Credentials

Go to GitHub Developer Settings and:

1. Create a new OAuth app.

2. Set the authorization callback URL to `http://localhost:3000/auth/github/callback`.

3. Copy the **Client ID** and **Client Secret**, and add them to `.env`:

ini

```
GITHUB_CLIENT_ID=your_github_client_id

GITHUB_CLIENT_SECRET=your_github_client_secret
```

3. Implementing GitHub OAuth with Passport.js

Modify `config/passport.js`:

javascript

```
const GitHubStrategy = require("passport-
github2").Strategy;

passport.use(new GitHubStrategy({

    clientID: process.env.GITHUB_CLIENT_ID,

    clientSecret:
process.env.GITHUB_CLIENT_SECRET,

    callbackURL: "/auth/github/callback"

}, (accessToken, refreshToken, profile, done)
=> {

    return done(null, profile);

}));
```

Modify `routes/authRoutes.js` to include GitHub authentication:

javascript

```
router.get("/github",
passport.authenticate("github",    {    scope:
["user:email"] }));

router.get("/github/callback",
passport.authenticate("github", {
```

```
    failureRedirect: "/login"

}), (req, res) => {

    res.redirect("/profile");

});
```

Now, visiting `http://localhost:3000/auth/github` will allow users to log in with GitHub.

Common Pitfalls and Debugging Tips

- **Invalid redirect URI error** – Ensure the callback URL matches what you configured in Google/GitHub settings.

- **Missing session data after login** – Make sure `express-session` is correctly set up before `passport.initialize()`.

- **User data not stored persistently** – In production, store user details in a database instead of the session.

Chapter 8: Error Handling, Logging, and Debugging

Picture this: You've just deployed your Express.js application to production. Everything looks fine—until users start reporting errors. One request results in a cryptic "500 Internal Server Error." Another request just hangs indefinitely. And worst of all? You have no idea why.

This is every developer's nightmare. Bugs are inevitable, but a well-structured error-handling and logging system can make the difference between a quick fix and hours of frustration.

In this chapter, we'll focus on three core aspects:

1. **Best practices for error handling in Express.js** – Catching and managing errors effectively.

2. **Implementing a global error-handling middleware** – Ensuring all errors are handled consistently.

3. **Using Winston and Morgan for logging** – Capturing and tracking issues before they escalate.

By the end, you'll have a solid strategy for handling errors, logging issues, and debugging your Express.js applications like a pro.

8.1 Best Practices for Error Handling in Express.js

Let's say you've just built an Express.js API that handles user authentication. Everything works fine in development, but once deployed, users start encountering issues. Some requests return a **500 Internal Server Error** with no explanation. Others fail silently, leaving users frustrated. Without proper error handling, debugging becomes a nightmare, and users are left in the dark.

Error handling is not just about catching bugs; it's about **ensuring your application fails gracefully**. A well-handled error informs developers what went wrong and guides users on what to do next. Poor error handling, on the other hand, can lead to **security vulnerabilities, poor user experience, and endless debugging sessions**.

In this section, we'll break down **best practices for handling errors in Express.js**, covering:

1. **Understanding Express.js error handling** and how middleware fits into the process.

2. **Using try-catch blocks effectively** in asynchronous functions to prevent unhandled promise rejections.

3. **Creating structured error responses** that provide meaningful feedback to users without exposing sensitive details.

4. **Custom error classes** for more granular error management.

5. **Handling errors globally** using middleware to keep error management centralized.

By the end of this section, you'll have a solid approach to handling errors in Express.js, making your applications **more resilient, maintainable, and user-friendly**.

Understanding How Express.js Handles Errors

Express follows a **middleware-based approach** to handling requests and responses. This applies to errors as well. By default, if an error occurs inside a route handler and isn't caught, Express will **crash** the application or return a generic **500 Internal Server Error**.

Consider this example:

javascript

```
app.get("/user/:id", async (req, res) => {

    const         user          =           await
getUserById(req.params.id);  //  What  if  this
fails?

    res.json(user);
```

```
});
```

If `getUserById` fails (e.g., the database is down), the request will **hang indefinitely**, and Express won't automatically know an error occurred. To prevent this, you need **explicit error handling**.

---

1. Using Try-Catch for Asynchronous Code

JavaScript's asynchronous nature makes error handling tricky. Errors inside `async/await` functions **don't get caught automatically** unless explicitly handled.

Here's a common mistake developers make:

javascript

```javascript
app.get("/data", async (req, res) => {

    const data = await fetchData(); // If fetchData fails, what happens?

    res.json(data);

});
```

If `fetchData` throws an error, the request will **never complete**, leaving the user waiting indefinitely. The fix? **Wrap asynchronous code in a try-catch block** and pass errors to the next middleware function:

javascript

```
app.get("/data", async (req, res, next) => {

    try {

        const data = await fetchData();

        res.json(data);

    } catch (error) {

        next(error); // Pass the error to
Express

    }

});
```

Using `next(error)` ensures Express **knows an error occurred** and will pass it to an error-handling middleware, preventing the app from crashing unexpectedly.

2. Avoiding Over-Exposing Errors to Users

When an error occurs, it's tempting to send the full error message to the client. But doing so can **expose sensitive information** about your application's internals.

Bad Practice: Exposing Technical Errors

javascript

```javascript
app.get("/profile", async (req, res, next) =>
{

    try {

        const       profile        =        await
getProfile(req.user.id);

        res.json(profile);

    } catch (error) {

        res.status(500).json({            error:
error.message });

    }

});
```

If a database error occurs, the response might look like this:

json

```json
{

    "error": "SequelizeDatabaseError: column
'password' does not exist"
```

```
}
```

This reveals implementation details **attackers could exploit**.

Best Practice: Send a Generic Error Message

Instead, return a **safe** error message while logging the actual error for debugging:

javascript

```javascript
app.get("/profile", async (req, res, next) =>
{
    try {
        const profile = await
getProfile(req.user.id);

        res.json(profile);
    } catch (error) {
        console.error(error); // Log the full
error

        res.status(500).json({      error:
"Something went wrong. Please try again
later." });
    }
```

```
});
```

This keeps the response **secure** while ensuring users aren't left clueless.

---

3. Creating Custom Error Classes

Instead of using plain Error objects, creating **custom error classes** provides more control over error handling.

Why Use Custom Errors?

- Helps differentiate different types of errors (e.g., validation errors vs. database errors).

- Allows setting custom status codes and structured responses.

- Makes debugging easier by categorizing errors.

Creating an AppError Class

javascript

```javascript
class AppError extends Error {

    constructor(message, statusCode) {

        super(message);
```

```
        this.statusCode = statusCode;

    }

}
```

Now, we can use it in routes:

javascript

```
app.get("/protected", (req, res, next) => {

    if (!req.user) {

        return                              next(new
AppError("Unauthorized access", 401));

    }

    res.json({ message: "Welcome!" });

});
```

This approach ensures that different errors can be
handled appropriately.

---

4. Implementing a Centralized Error
Handler

Manually handling errors in each route is tedious. Instead, Express allows defining a **global error-handling middleware** to catch all errors in one place.

Creating an Error Middleware

Create a file `middleware/errorHandler.js`:

javascript

```javascript
const errorHandler = (err, req, res, next) => {

    console.error(err.stack);


    res.status(err.statusCode || 500).json({
        error: err.message || "Internal Server Error"
    });
};


module.exports = errorHandler;
```

Using the Middleware in Express

In `server.js`, register it **after all routes**:

javascript

```javascript
const express = require("express");

const app = express();

const errorHandler = require("./middleware/errorHandler");

app.use("/api", require("./routes/apiRoutes"));

// Global error handler (must be last)

app.use(errorHandler);

app.listen(3000, () => console.log("Server running on port 3000"));
```

Now, any unhandled errors will be **automatically caught and handled**, keeping your application stable and maintainable.

Writing Resilient Express Apps

By now, you've learned **best practices for handling errors in Express.js**, including:

- Using **try-catch** for handling asynchronous errors properly.

- Avoiding **exposing sensitive error messages** to users.

- Creating **custom error classes** for better error management.

- Implementing a **global error-handling middleware** to centralize error handling.

These techniques will **help you build robust Express.js applications that fail gracefully**, making debugging easier and ensuring a better experience for users.

Next Steps:

- Integrate a logging library like **Winston** to track errors in production.

- Add **error tracking tools** like Sentry for real-time error monitoring.

- Implement **rate limiting** to protect your API from excessive error-triggering requests.

8.2 Implementing Global Error Handling Middleware

Imagine this: You've built a robust Express.js API, handling errors in each route with `try-catch` blocks. Everything seems fine—until your app starts growing. More routes, more handlers, and suddenly, every endpoint has redundant error-handling code cluttering your logic.

Not only does this make your code messy, but it also **introduces inconsistencies**. Some routes return detailed error messages, while others just fail silently. Debugging becomes frustrating because errors aren't logged uniformly, and worst of all, users get confusing responses that don't help them understand what went wrong.

This is where **global error handling middleware** comes in. Instead of handling errors manually in every route, Express allows us to define a centralized **error-handling middleware**. This middleware acts as a **catch-all** for unhandled errors, ensuring they are logged, structured, and returned properly.

In this section, we'll cover:

- **How Express routes pass errors** to middleware.

- **How to create a centralized error-handling middleware** to streamline error management.

- **Logging and debugging best practices** to make troubleshooting easier.

- **Ensuring security by handling errors safely** without exposing sensitive details.

By the end, your Express application will be **more maintainable, resilient, and easier to debug**.

1. How Express Passes Errors to Middleware

Express follows a **middleware-based** approach to handling both requests and errors. Any function that has (err, req, res, next) as its parameters is considered an **error-handling middleware**.

Whenever an error occurs inside a route handler or another middleware, it can be passed to Express's built-in error-handling flow using next(error).

Example: Manual Error Handling in Each Route (Bad Practice)

Consider a simple API that fetches user data:

javascript

```
app.get("/user/:id", async (req, res) => {

    try {

        const user = await
getUserById(req.params.id);

        if (!user) {

            return res.status(404).json({
error: "User not found" });

        }

        res.json(user);

    } catch (error) {
```

```
        console.error(error);

        res.status(500).json({            error:
"Something went wrong" });

    }

});
```

Here's the problem:

- Every route needs its own `try-catch` block.

- Errors aren't handled consistently across routes.

- If we forget to catch an error, the app **could crash**.

Instead, we should **delegate error handling to a global middleware**.

---

2. Creating a Global Error Handling Middleware

Instead of cluttering every route with error-handling logic, Express allows defining **one centralized function** that catches all errors.

Step 1: Define the Error Middleware

Create a new file: `middleware/errorHandler.js`

javascript

```javascript
const errorHandler = (err, req, res, next) =>
{

    console.error(err.stack);  // Log  error
stack for debugging

    const statusCode = err.statusCode || 500;

    const message = err.message || "Internal
Server Error";

    res.status(statusCode).json({

        success: false,

        error: message,

    });

};

module.exports = errorHandler;
```

Step 2: Register the Middleware in Express

In server.js or app.js, register the middleware **after
all routes**:

javascript

```javascript
const express = require("express");

const app = express();
```

```javascript
const          errorHandler          =
require("./middleware/errorHandler");

app.use("/api",
require("./routes/apiRoutes"));

// Global error handler (must be last)

app.use(errorHandler);

app.listen(3000, () => console.log("Server
running on port 3000"));
```

Now, instead of handling errors in every route, simply use `next(error)`, and the middleware will handle the response.

---

3. Using Custom Error Classes for Better Error Control

A global error handler is useful, but **not all errors should be treated the same way**. Some might be user-related (e.g., invalid input), while others are server errors.

To manage different error types, define a **custom error class**:

javascript

```javascript
class AppError extends Error {
```

```javascript
    constructor(message, statusCode) {

        super(message);

        this.statusCode = statusCode;

    }

}
```

Now, throw custom errors in your routes:

javascript

```javascript
app.get("/protected", (req, res, next) => {

    if (!req.user) {

        return                          next(new
AppError("Unauthorized access", 401));

    }

    res.json({ message: "Welcome!" });

});
```

Modify the error handler to recognize AppError:

javascript

```javascript
const errorHandler = (err, req, res, next) =>
{
```

```javascript
    console.error(err.stack);

    const statusCode = err.statusCode || 500;

    const message = err instanceof AppError ?
err.message : "Internal Server Error";


    res.status(statusCode).json({

        success: false,

        error: message,

    });

};
```

Now, controlled errors return **meaningful messages**, while unknown errors return a generic **500 Internal Server Error** to avoid exposing sensitive details.

4. Logging Errors for Debugging

Logging errors properly is crucial for debugging, especially in production. Instead of `console.error()`, use a logging library like **Winston** to store errors in log files.

Install Winston

bash

```bash
npm install winston
```

Set Up Logging in `logger.js`

javascript

```javascript
const { createLogger, format, transports } =
require("winston");

const logger = createLogger({

    level: "error",

    format: format.combine(

        format.timestamp(),

        format.json()

    ),

    transports: [

        new    transports.File({    filename:
"errors.log" }),

        new transports.Console()

    ],

});
```

```javascript
module.exports = logger;
```

Update Error Handler to Use Winston

javascript

```javascript
const logger = require("../utils/logger");


const errorHandler = (err, req, res, next) => {

    logger.error(`${err.message}        -
${req.method} ${req.url}`);


    res.status(err.statusCode || 500).json({

        success: false,

        error: err.message || "Internal Server
Error",

    });

};
```

Now, errors are **logged to a file** and **printed to the console**, making debugging easier.

---

5. Best Practices for Secure Error Handling

To ensure your error handling is robust and secure, follow these best practices:

1. Never Expose Internal Errors to Users

Instead of sending raw error messages, always return **safe, user-friendly messages**.

2. Use a Structured Error Format

Consistently return structured JSON responses:

```json
{
    "success": false,
    "error": "User not found"
}
```

3. Log Errors but Don't Leak Sensitive Data

- Use Winston or a logging service.

- Avoid logging user credentials, API keys, or sensitive details.

4. Handle Uncaught Exceptions and Rejections

For errors outside Express, handle them globally:

javascript

```javascript
process.on("uncaughtException", (err) => {

    console.error("Uncaught        Exception:",
err);

});


process.on("unhandledRejection",        (reason,
promise) => {

    console.error("Unhandled        Rejection:",
reason);

});
```

Writing Resilient Express Applications

By implementing a **global error-handling middleware**, you've transformed error management from **messy and inconsistent** to **organized and scalable**.

Key takeaways:

- **Centralize error handling** using Express middleware.

- **Use custom error classes** to differentiate error types.

- **Log errors efficiently** with Winston.

- **Handle async errors properly** using `next(error)`.

- **Secure your error responses** by hiding internal details.

With these best practices, your Express.js application is now **more robust, easier to debug, and production-ready**.

Next Steps:

- Integrate an error-tracking tool like **Sentry**.

- Implement **rate limiting** to prevent excessive error-triggering requests.

- Improve user experience by adding **custom error pages** for front-end applications.

8.3 Using Winston and Morgan for Logging

Imagine you've just launched your Express.js application. Everything seems fine—until users start reporting errors, performance slows down, and you have no idea what's causing the issues. Debugging becomes a nightmare because there's no record of what's happening under the hood.

This is where logging comes in.

Logging is more than just printing messages to the console; it's about **tracking requests, capturing errors, monitoring performance, and gaining insights** into your application's behavior. Without proper logging, diagnosing issues in production can feel like searching for a needle in a haystack.

In this chapter, we'll explore two essential tools for logging in Express:

- **Morgan** – A lightweight logging middleware for tracking HTTP requests.

- **Winston** – A powerful logging library for structured, persistent logs.

By the end of this chapter, you'll know how to:

- Log HTTP requests efficiently using Morgan.

- Set up Winston for structured logging.

- Save logs to files for debugging and monitoring.

- Implement logging best practices to keep your app maintainable and scalable.

---

1. Logging HTTP Requests with Morgan

The Need for Request Logging

Every time a user interacts with your API, they send HTTP requests. Knowing what requests are being made, how long they take, and if they succeed or fail is crucial for monitoring and debugging.

Morgan is a simple yet powerful middleware that logs details about incoming requests, such as:

- HTTP method (GET, POST, etc.)

- Request URL

- Response status code

- Response time

Installing Morgan

To use Morgan in your Express application, install it via npm:

bash

```
npm install morgan
```

Basic Usage

To enable request logging, add Morgan as middleware in your app.js or server.js:

javascript

```
const express = require("express");

const morgan = require("morgan");
```

```
const app = express();

// Use Morgan with the 'dev' format for
detailed logs

app.use(morgan("dev"));

app.get("/", (req, res) => {

    res.send("Hello, world!");

});



app.listen(3000, () => console.log("Server
running on port 3000"));
```

Now, whenever you make a request, Morgan will log details in the console:

sql

```
GET / 200 5.234 ms
```

The dev format provides colored, concise logs useful for development.

2. Customizing Morgan for Production Logging

Using the 'combined' Format

In production, logs need to be more structured. The `combined` format follows Apache-style logging, which includes:

- Remote client IP

- Request method and URL

- Response status

- User-agent (browser, device, etc.)

To enable it:

javascript

```javascript
app.use(morgan("combined"));
```

A typical log entry would look like this:

swift

```swift
192.168.1.1 - - [28/Mar/2025:12:34:56 +0000]
"GET /home HTTP/1.1" 200 512 "Mozilla/5.0"
```

This level of detail is helpful for tracking traffic patterns and debugging API issues.

Saving Logs to a File

For long-term storage and analysis, write logs to a file instead of the console:

javascript

```
const fs = require("fs");

const path = require("path");

const         logStream         =
fs.createWriteStream(path.join(__dirname,
"access.log"), { flags: "a" });

app.use(morgan("combined", { stream: logStream
}));
```

Now, all HTTP requests will be stored in `access.log`.

---

3. Implementing Application Logging with Winston

Why Use Winston?

While Morgan logs HTTP requests, Winston provides **structured logging** for everything else—errors, database queries, API calls, and custom application events.

Winston allows you to:

- Log messages at different levels (info, warn, error).

- Format logs for better readability.

- Write logs to multiple destinations (console, files, external services).

Installing Winston

bash

```
npm install winston
```

Setting Up a Logger

Create a new file: utils/logger.js

javascript

```
const { createLogger, format, transports } =
require("winston");


const logger = createLogger({

    level: "info",   // Default log level

    format: format.combine(

        format.timestamp(),

        format.json()

    ),

    transports: [
```

```
        new transports.Console(),

        new     transports.File({     filename:
"app.log" }),

    ],

});


module.exports = logger;
```

This logger:

- Logs **info-level and above** messages.

- Stores logs in `app.log`.

- Includes timestamps for better tracking.

---

4. Using Winston in Express

Logging Errors

Modify your global error handler to log errors using Winston:

javascript

```
const logger = require("../utils/logger");
```

```
const errorHandler = (err, req, res, next) =>
{

    logger.error(`${err.message}          -
${req.method} ${req.url}`);


    res.status(err.statusCode || 500).json({

        success: false,

        error: err.message || "Internal Server
Error",

    });

};
```

Now, every error will be logged with its message, HTTP method, and URL.

Example log entry:

json

```
{

    "level": "error",

    "message":   "User   not   found   -   GET
/users/123",

    "timestamp": "2025-03-28T12:00:00Z"
```

```
}
```

Logging Custom Events

To log a custom event, use:

javascript

```javascript
logger.info("User logged in", { userId: 123
});
```

This keeps logs structured and searchable.

---

5. Best Practices for Logging in Express

1. Separate HTTP and Application Logs

Use **Morgan** for request logging and **Winston** for application-specific logs.

2. Use Log Levels Properly

- `info` – General events (e.g., "User registered")

- `warn` – Unusual but non-fatal conditions (e.g., "Slow database response")

- error – Critical issues that need attention (e.g., "Database connection failed")

3. Avoid Logging Sensitive Data

Never log passwords, API keys, or personal user data.

4. Rotate Logs to Prevent Large Files

Use a log rotation package like winston-daily-rotate-file to prevent logs from growing indefinitely.

bash

```
npm install winston-daily-rotate-file
```

Configure Winston to rotate logs daily:

javascript

```
const DailyRotateFile = require("winston-daily-rotate-file");

const transport = new DailyRotateFile({
    filename: "logs/app-%DATE%.log",
    datePattern: "YYYY-MM-DD",
    maxFiles: "14d",
});

logger.add(transport);
```

Now, logs will be automatically rotated every day and kept for 14 days.

Building a Reliable Logging System

By integrating **Morgan and Winston**, you've built a **robust logging system** that:

- **Tracks incoming requests** with Morgan.

- **Logs structured application events** with Winston.

- **Persists logs to files** for long-term analysis.

- **Ensures security and efficiency** with best practices.

With these logging techniques in place, debugging and monitoring your Express application will be much easier.

Next Steps:

- Integrate an error-tracking tool like **Sentry**.

- Use **log analysis tools** like ELK Stack or Datadog for insights.

- Implement **real-time monitoring** for performance tracking.

Chapter 9: Session Management and Caching

Imagine you're building an e-commerce platform. A user logs in, adds items to their cart, and navigates to checkout—only to find their cart has mysteriously emptied. Frustrating, right? Without proper session management, user data is lost between requests.

Now, let's say your site has grown, and thousands of users are browsing at the same time. Your database is working overtime fetching the same product details repeatedly. This slows everything down, frustrating users and increasing costs.

Sessions and caching help solve these problems.

- **Sessions** ensure user data persists across multiple requests, making authentication, shopping carts, and personalization possible.

- **Caching** stores frequently accessed data in memory, reducing database queries and improving response times.

In this chapter, we'll cover:

- How to **implement sessions in Express.js** to track user state.

- How to **use Redis for session storage** to handle high traffic.

- How to **improve performance with caching** strategies.

By the end, you'll be able to build faster, more reliable applications that handle sessions and caching effectively.

9.1 Implementing Sessions with Express.js

Imagine you're building a web application with user authentication. A user logs in, but after clicking to another page, they are suddenly logged out. They try adding an item to their shopping cart, but when they navigate away, the cart is empty. If you've run into this, you've hit one of the biggest limitations of HTTP—it's stateless.

Every request a client makes is independent, meaning the server doesn't remember anything between them. This is a problem when building applications that require user authentication, shopping carts, or any kind of user-specific interaction.

This is where **sessions** come in.

Sessions allow us to store user-related data **between requests**, giving the illusion of continuity. When a user logs in, their session persists even when they navigate through different pages. Instead of asking them to log in every time they visit a new route, we store their session data on the server and identify them with a unique session ID.

In this section, we'll cover:

- How sessions work in Express.js

- Setting up `express-session` to persist user data

- Storing session data in memory and databases

- Best practices and security considerations

By the end, you'll have a working session-based authentication system and a solid understanding of how sessions help maintain user state in modern web applications.

Understanding Sessions in Express.js

How Sessions Work

Sessions rely on a simple mechanism:

1. A user logs in or interacts with the app.

2. The server creates a **session object** and assigns it a unique **session ID**.

3. The session ID is stored in a **cookie** on the user's browser.

4. On each subsequent request, the session ID is sent to the server.

5. The server retrieves the associated session data and restores the user's state.

Unlike **cookies**, which store all data in the client's browser, **sessions keep data on the server**, reducing exposure to security risks.

Setting Up express-session

Express.js doesn't manage sessions out of the box, so we need the `express-session` middleware. Install it with:

bash

```
npm install express-session
```

Then, configure it in your Express app:

javascript

```
const express = require("express");

const session = require("express-session");

const app = express();

app.use(session({

    secret: "supersecretkey",

    resave: false,

    saveUninitialized: true,

    cookie: { secure: false } // Set to true
if using HTTPS
```

```
}));


app.get("/", (req, res) => {

    req.session.views = (req.session.views ||
0) + 1;

    res.send(`You    have    visited    this    page
${req.session.views} times`);

});

app.listen(3000,    ()    =>    console.log("Server
running on port 3000"));
```

Breaking Down the Code

- secret: Used to sign session cookies,
  preventing tampering. This should be a strong,
  unpredictable string.

- resave: Prevents sessions from being saved if
  they haven't changed.

- saveUninitialized: Saves new sessions that
  haven't been modified.

- cookie.secure: Ensures cookies are only sent
  over HTTPS (set true in production).

If you run the server and refresh the page, you'll see the session counter increase—your Express app is now tracking session data.

Storing User Data in Sessions

Sessions are useful for storing temporary user-specific data, such as authentication status. Let's create an authentication system that remembers logged-in users.

User Login with Sessions

We'll simulate a login system where users authenticate with a username.

javascript

```javascript
app.use(express.json());

app.post("/login", (req, res) => {

    const { username } = req.body;

    if (!username) {

        return res.status(400).send("Username is required");

    }

    req.session.user = { username };

    res.send(`Welcome, ${username}! Your session has started.`);
```

288

```javascript
});

app.get("/profile", (req, res) => {

    if (!req.session.user) {

        return
res.status(401).send("Unauthorized.    Please
log in.");

    }

    res.send(`Hello,
${req.session.user.username}.  This  is  your
profile.`);

});
```

Logging Out and Destroying Sessions

To clear session data, we can use
`req.session.destroy()`.

javascript

```javascript
app.post("/logout", (req, res) => {

    req.session.destroy(err => {

        if (err) {

            return
res.status(500).send("Error logging out");

        }
```

289

```
        res.send("Logged out successfully");

    });

});
```

Testing the Authentication Flow

1. Start the server.

2. Use Postman or `curl` to send a `POST` request to `/login` with `{ "username": "john_doe" }`.

3. Visit `/profile`—you should see your username.

4. Call `/logout`, then try `/profile` again; it should return an unauthorized message.

Handling Session Persistence

By default, `express-session` stores session data in memory, meaning sessions disappear when the server restarts. For real-world applications, we use **persistent session stores**, such as **Redis** or databases.

Using Redis for Session Storage

Redis is a popular in-memory key-value store that improves session management by making it **persistent, scalable, and fast**.

Install Redis and the required dependencies:

bash

```bash
npm install redis connect-redis express-session
```

Then, configure Redis as the session store:

javascript

```javascript
const Redis = require("ioredis");
const RedisStore = require("connect-redis").default;

const redisClient = new Redis();

app.use(session({
    store: new RedisStore({ client: redisClient }),
    secret: "supersecretkey",
    resave: false,
    saveUninitialized: false,
```

```
    cookie: { secure: false }

}));
```

Now, session data persists across server restarts, making your authentication system more reliable.

Best Practices for Session Management

1. Use Secure Cookies in Production

Set `cookie.secure = true` to ensure session cookies are only transmitted over HTTPS.

2. Set an Expiry Time for Sessions

Automatically remove old sessions by setting a session timeout:

javascript

```javascript
app.use(session({

    secret: "supersecretkey",

    resave: false,

    saveUninitialized: false,

    cookie: { secure: false, maxAge: 600000 }
// Expires in 10 minutes

}));
```

3. Avoid Storing Sensitive Data in Sessions

Sessions should store only non-sensitive user data. Never store passwords or API keys.

4. Use a Session Store for Scalability

For large applications, always use Redis or a database-backed session store instead of memory storage.

Bringing It All Together

In this section, you've learned how to:

- Implement **sessions in Express.js** to maintain user state.

- Store user authentication data in sessions.

- **Destroy sessions** when logging out.

- **Use Redis for session persistence** to handle high-traffic applications.

- Follow **best practices** for secure session management.

Sessions are essential for building dynamic, user-friendly web applications. However, they are just one piece of the puzzle. In the next section, we'll explore **how to improve performance with caching strategies**, ensuring your app remains fast and scalable as it grows.

9.2 Using Redis for Session Storage

Imagine you've built a robust Express.js application with user authentication and dynamic content. During development, you used the default in-memory session storage provided by `express-session`. Everything works great—until you deploy your app to production. Suddenly, you face two major issues: sessions are lost when the server restarts, and memory usage skyrockets as more users interact with your app.

This is where Redis comes into play. Redis is an in-memory data structure store known for its speed and persistence options. By using Redis for session storage, you can overcome the limitations of in-memory storage, ensure session data survives server restarts, and support scalable, distributed architectures. In this chapter, we'll explore how to integrate Redis with Express.js to manage sessions efficiently.

Why Redis for Session Storage?

Traditional in-memory session storage is sufficient for development or small-scale applications, but it comes with significant drawbacks in production:

- **Volatility:** Sessions stored in memory are lost if the server restarts.

- **Scalability:** In-memory storage does not work well when deploying multiple instances behind a load balancer.

- **Memory Consumption:** Large numbers of sessions can quickly exhaust available memory.

Redis addresses these issues by offering a fast, persistent, and distributed solution. It keeps session data in memory for rapid access while providing options to persist data to disk. Additionally, Redis supports clustering and replication, making it an excellent choice for applications that need to scale.

Setting Up Redis in Your Express.js Application

1. Installing Redis and Connect-Redis

Before integrating Redis, you need to install it on your system. You can download and install Redis from the official Redis website. Once installed, start the Redis server using the default configuration.

Next, add the necessary packages to your project:

bash

```
npm install redis connect-redis express-session
```

- **redis**: A Redis client for Node.js.

- **connect-redis**: A Redis session store for Express.

- **express-session**: Session middleware for Express.

2. Configuring Express to Use Redis for Session Storage

Create or update your session configuration in your Express app. Typically, this is done in your main application file (e.g., server.js or app.js). Here's how to set it up:

javascript

```javascript
const express = require("express");

const session = require("express-session");

const Redis = require("ioredis");

const RedisStore = require("connect-redis").default;

require("dotenv").config();

const app = express();

// Initialize Redis client

const redisClient = new Redis({

    host: process.env.REDIS_HOST || "127.0.0.1",
```

```
  port: process.env.REDIS_PORT || 6379

});


// Configure session middleware to use
RedisStore

app.use(session({

    store:    new    RedisStore({    client:
redisClient }),

    secret:   process.env.SESSION_SECRET   ||
"supersecretkey",

    resave: false,

    saveUninitialized: false,

    cookie: { secure: false, maxAge: 600000 }
// 10 minutes for development; set secure:true
in production with HTTPS

}));


app.get("/", (req, res) => {

    // Simple demonstration of session usage

    req.session.views = (req.session.views ||
0) + 1;
```

```
    res.send(`You    have    visited    this    page
${req.session.views} times`);

});

const PORT = process.env.PORT || 3000;

app.listen(PORT,    ()    =>    console.log(`Server
running on port ${PORT}`));
```

Breaking Down the Code:

- **Redis Client:**
  We use the `ioredis` package to connect to Redis. The host and port are configurable via environment variables.

- **Session Store:**
  `connect-redis` is used to create a Redis-backed session store. This replaces the default in-memory store, ensuring sessions are stored in Redis.

- **Session Configuration:**

  - `secret`: A secret key used to sign the session ID cookie.

  - `resave` and `saveUninitialized`: Settings that prevent unnecessary session saves.

  - `cookie`: Configurable options, such as `maxAge` (session duration) and `secure` (ensuring cookies are sent only over

HTTPS in production).

Testing Your Redis-Backed Sessions

Run your Express.js application and navigate to the root route. Each time you refresh the page, the session count should increment. Even if you restart your server, as long as Redis is running and properly configured, session data should persist.

Best Practices for Using Redis for Session Storage

1. Environment-Specific Configuration

- **Use Environment Variables:**
  Keep configuration settings like Redis host, port, and session secrets in environment variables. This practice improves security and makes your app more flexible across different environments (development, staging, production).

- **Secure Cookies in Production:**
  Ensure that the `cookie.secure` option is set to `true` in production environments, so cookies are only sent over HTTPS.

2. Session Expiration and Cleanup

- **Set a Reasonable Session Expiry:**
  The `maxAge` property on the session cookie

controls how long a session lasts. Choose a duration that balances user convenience with security.

- **Enable Redis Persistence:**
  Configure Redis to persist data on disk using snapshots (RDB) or append-only files (AOF) to prevent data loss during server restarts.

3. Scaling Your Application

- **Redis Clustering:**
  For high-traffic applications, consider using Redis clusters. This distributes the session load across multiple Redis nodes, improving reliability and performance.

- **Monitoring and Logging:**
  Implement monitoring for your Redis instance to keep track of performance, memory usage, and any potential issues. Tools like Redis Sentinel can help with failover and high availability.

Enhancing User Experience with Persistent Sessions

Implementing Redis for session storage is a critical step in building scalable, reliable web applications with Express.js. By offloading session data from the server's memory to Redis, you ensure that:

- Sessions persist across server restarts.

- Your application can scale horizontally in a distributed environment.

- User data is handled securely and efficiently.

In this chapter, we learned how to:

- Install and configure Redis and connect-redis.

- Set up `express-session` to use Redis as a session store.

- Apply best practices such as using environment variables, securing cookies, and planning for scalability.

Next Steps:

- Experiment with session management by integrating Redis into an existing project.

- Explore advanced Redis features like clustering and persistence.

- Monitor your Redis instance in production to ensure optimal performance.

By following these practices, you'll build a more robust application that delivers a seamless user experience while maintaining high performance and scalability.

9.3 Improving Performance with Caching Strategies

Every millisecond counts when it comes to web performance. Imagine a scenario where your Express.js application serves dynamic content, such as product listings, user dashboards, or API responses. As your user base grows, your database queries and API calls start piling up, slowing down response times. The result? Frustrated users, higher server costs, and potential loss of business.

This is where caching comes into play. A well-implemented caching strategy can dramatically improve performance by reducing redundant computations and database queries. By temporarily storing frequently accessed data, your application can serve users faster while decreasing the load on your backend systems. In this chapter, we'll explore different caching techniques in Express.js and how to leverage Redis to make your app more efficient.

Understanding Caching: Why It Matters

Caching is the practice of storing copies of frequently used data in a fast-access location, reducing the need to fetch it from a slower data source. Here's why caching is crucial for web applications:

1. **Reduced Latency** – Cached data is retrieved much faster than querying a database or

making an external API call.

2. **Lower Server Load** – By serving responses from cache, you reduce the number of database queries and computations.

3. **Improved Scalability** – A caching layer allows your application to handle more requests without increasing server costs.

4. **Better User Experience** – Faster response times lead to happier users and better engagement.

Caching can be implemented at multiple levels:

- **Client-Side Caching** (e.g., browser cache, service workers)

- **Application-Level Caching** (e.g., in-memory caching within Express)

- **Database Query Caching** (e.g., Redis, Memcached)

- **CDN Caching** (e.g., Cloudflare, AWS CloudFront)

In this chapter, we'll focus on application-level caching using Redis.

Implementing Caching in an Express.js Application

1. Installing and Setting Up Redis for Caching

Before implementing caching, ensure you have Redis installed and running. If Redis isn't installed, you can download it from Redis.io and start the server:

bash

```
redis-server
```

Now, install the necessary packages in your Express.js project:

bash

```
npm install redis express
```

Next, set up Redis in your application:

javascript

```
const express = require("express");
const Redis = require("ioredis");
require("dotenv").config();
```

```javascript
const app = express();

const redisClient = new Redis({

    host:        process.env.REDIS_HOST       ||
"127.0.0.1",

    port: process.env.REDIS_PORT || 6379

});
```

2. Caching API Responses

Let's say you have an API endpoint that fetches data from an external source or a database. Without caching, every request triggers a new database query, which can be slow. Instead, let's cache the response in Redis.

javascript

```javascript
app.get("/products", async (req, res) => {

    try {

        const cacheKey = "products";


        // Check if data exists in Redis
```

```javascript
    const    cachedData    =    await
redisClient.get(cacheKey);

    if (cachedData) {

        console.log("Serving        from
cache");

        return
res.json(JSON.parse(cachedData));

    }


    // Simulate database query (replace
with real DB call)
    const products = [

        { id: 1, name: "Laptop", price:
1200 },

        { id: 2, name: "Phone", price: 800
}

    ];


    // Store data in Redis with an
expiration time (e.g., 60 seconds)

    await redisClient.setex(cacheKey, 60,
JSON.stringify(products));
```

```
        console.log("Serving from database");

        res.json(products);

    } catch (error) {

        console.error("Error        fetching
products:", error);

        res.status(500).send("Internal Server
Error");

    }

});
```

Breaking Down the Code:

- **Check if data exists in Redis.** If cached data is found, return it immediately.

- **If not cached, fetch from the database.** In this example, we use a static array, but in a real-world scenario, this would be a database call.

- **Store the response in Redis.** The `setex` method stores data with an expiration time (60 seconds in this case).

- **Return the data to the user.** Whether from cache or the database, the response remains the same.

3. Expiring and Invalidating Cached Data

One challenge with caching is ensuring that outdated data doesn't persist. Here's how to handle expiration and invalidation:

- **Set an expiration time (`setex`)** – Automatically removes old data after a specified duration.

- **Manually delete cache on updates (`del`)** – When data changes, remove the old cache entry.

For example, if we have an API that updates product prices, we should clear the cache:

javascript

```javascript
app.post("/update-product/:id", async (req, res) => {

    try {

        const productId = req.params.id;

        const updatedProduct = { id: productId, name: "Laptop", price: 1000 };


        // Update the database (simulate with a success message)
```

```
        console.log("Product      updated      in
database");


        // Invalidate the cache

        await redisClient.del("products");


        res.json({ message: "Product updated",
updatedProduct });
    } catch (error) {

        console.error("Error           updating
product:", error);

        res.status(500).send("Internal  Server
Error");

    }
});
```

Every time a product is updated, the cache is cleared, ensuring the next request fetches fresh data.

Advanced Caching Strategies

1. Cache-Aside Strategy

Also known as lazy loading, this strategy fetches data from the cache if available; otherwise, it loads data from the database and updates the cache. This is the approach we used in the `/products` API example.

2. Write-Through Caching

With this method, data is written to the cache **and** the database simultaneously. This ensures the cache always has fresh data.

javascript

```javascript
app.post("/add-product", async (req, res) => {

    const newProduct = { id: 3, name: "Tablet", price: 500 };

    // Simulate database insert

    console.log("Product added to database");


    // Update cache immediately

    const cachedProducts = await redisClient.get("products");

    if (cachedProducts) {

        const products = JSON.parse(cachedProducts);

        products.push(newProduct);

        await redisClient.setex("products", 60, JSON.stringify(products));
```

```
    }
```

```
    res.json({   message:   "Product   added",
newProduct });
```

```
});
```

3. Least Recently Used (LRU) Eviction

Redis supports eviction policies to remove old data when memory is full. Setting an LRU policy ensures frequently accessed items stay in cache while rarely used ones are evicted.

To enable LRU eviction, configure Redis:

bash

```
redis-cli config set maxmemory-policy allkeys-
lru
```

Conclusion: The Power of Caching in Express.js

In this chapter, we explored how caching can significantly improve performance in Express.js applications by:

- **Reducing database load** through efficient data storage in Redis.

- **Speeding up responses** with in-memory caching.

- **Ensuring fresh data** by handling cache expiration and invalidation.

We implemented practical caching strategies like **cache-aside** and **write-through caching**, demonstrating how to balance performance and data consistency.

Next Steps:

- Experiment with caching other types of data (e.g., user authentication states, API responses).

- Use Redis monitoring tools to analyze cache efficiency.

- Explore advanced caching mechanisms like Redis clustering for high scalability.

By integrating caching effectively, your Express.js application will not only perform better but also scale efficiently, delivering a seamless experience to users.

PART 4: REAL-WORLD PROJECTS AND DEPLOYMENT

Chapter 10: Building a Full-Stack Blog Application (Hands-On Project)

If you've ever read a blog online, whether a tech article, a personal diary, or a company update, you've interacted with a system that combines a backend API, a frontend UI, and a database. Building a blog application is a classic full-stack project that helps you master essential web development concepts—API design, frontend-backend communication, and CRUD (Create, Read, Update, Delete) operations.

In this chapter, we'll walk through the process of creating a fully functional blog application using **Express.js for the backend**, a **MongoDB database**, and a **frontend built with a modern JavaScript framework**. This hands-on project will simulate real-world scenarios like handling user-generated content, structuring API endpoints efficiently, and connecting a frontend to an Express.js-powered backend.

By the end, you'll have a solid foundation for building and deploying full-stack applications, whether personal projects or production-grade systems. Let's dive in.

10.1 Setting Up the Project

The First Step in Building a Real-World Application

Every well-built web application starts with a solid foundation. When you're developing a full-stack project like a blog, setting up your backend correctly is crucial. A poorly structured backend can lead to performance issues, security vulnerabilities, and difficulty in scaling.

Think about a scenario where you're building a personal blogging platform. You need a system where users can write, edit, and delete posts, and those posts need to be stored in a database and retrieved efficiently. To make this work, we need an API that can handle CRUD (Create, Read, Update, Delete) operations. This is where Express.js comes in—it provides a lightweight and efficient way to build a backend that can handle these operations seamlessly.

Before diving into features like authentication, comments, or rich text formatting, we first need a working backend that connects to a database, handles requests, and serves data to a frontend. In this section, we'll set up our **Express.js backend**, configure a **MongoDB database**, and lay the groundwork for our **blog application API**.

Setting Up the Project Directory

The first step in any Express.js project is creating a structured folder layout. Instead of dumping everything into one file, we'll separate concerns from the start.

Begin by creating a new project directory and navigating into it:

bash

```
mkdir express-blog
```

```
cd express-blog
```

Now, initialize a Node.js project:

bash

```
npm init -y
```

This command creates a `package.json` file, which acts as a blueprint for our project's dependencies and scripts. The `-y` flag automatically applies default settings, so you won't need to answer setup prompts.

Installing Dependencies

An Express.js project typically requires several core dependencies. Let's install the necessary packages:

bash

```
npm install express mongoose dotenv cors body-parser
```

Here's a quick breakdown of what each package does:

- **express** – The backend framework that handles HTTP requests and responses.

- **mongoose** – An ODM (Object Data Modeling) library that allows us to interact with MongoDB in a structured way.

- **dotenv** – Loads environment variables from a `.env` file, keeping sensitive data like database credentials secure.

- **cors** – Enables Cross-Origin Resource Sharing, which allows our frontend to communicate with the backend.

- **body-parser** – Parses incoming JSON requests so our API can handle data sent from the frontend.

Once installed, you should see a `node_modules` folder and a `package-lock.json` file inside your project directory. These files store information about dependencies and their versions.

Setting Up the Express.js Server

Now, let's create the main entry point for our backend. Inside the project directory, create a new file named `index.js` and open it in a text editor.

javascript

```
require("dotenv").config();

const express = require("express");

const mongoose = require("mongoose");

const cors = require("cors");
```

```
const app = express();

const PORT = process.env.PORT || 5000;


// Middleware

app.use(express.json());

app.use(cors());


// Basic route

app.get("/", (req, res) => {

    res.send("Welcome to the Express.js Blog
API");

});


// Start the server

app.listen(PORT, () => {

    console.log(`Server    running    on    port
${PORT}`);

});
```

Breaking Down the Code

- We import `express`, `mongoose`, `dotenv`, and `cors`.

- We initialize an Express app and define a `PORT` variable that defaults to `5000` if not specified in `.env`.

- Middleware is added using `app.use()`. `express.json()` allows us to handle JSON data, and `cors()` enables cross-origin requests.

- We define a simple route (`/`) that returns a welcome message.

- Finally, we start the server with `app.listen()`, which makes our API accessible.

Run the server using:

bash

```
node index.js
```

If everything is set up correctly, you should see:

arduino

```
Server running on port 5000
```

Connecting to MongoDB

A blog application needs a database to store posts, and MongoDB is an excellent choice due to its flexibility and JSON-like document structure.

1. Installing MongoDB Locally (Optional)

If you don't have MongoDB installed, you can download it from MongoDB's official website. Alternatively, you can use **MongoDB Atlas**, a cloud-hosted version, which is easier for beginners.

2. Setting Up a `.env` File

To keep sensitive information out of our source code, create a `.env` file in the project root and add the following:

bash

```
MONGO_URI=mongodb://localhost:27017/express_b
log
```

Replace this with your MongoDB Atlas connection string if using a cloud database.

3. Connecting to MongoDB in Express.js

Modify `index.js` to establish a database connection:

javascript

```
mongoose.connect(process.env.MONGO_URI, {
```

320

```
    useNewUrlParser: true,

    useUnifiedTopology: true,
})

.then(() => console.log("MongoDB connected"))

.catch(err       =>       console.error("Database
connection error:", err));
```

4. Testing the Connection

Restart your server:

bash

```
node index.js
```

If everything is set up correctly, you should see:

arduino

```
MongoDB connected
Server running on port 5000
```

If you encounter connection errors, double-check your `.env` file, ensure MongoDB is running, and verify that your connection string is correct.

Project Structure Best Practices

Instead of keeping everything in `index.js`, it's best to follow a structured approach. Here's how our project structure will look as we expand the application:

bash

```
express-blog/

|— models/        # Database models (e.g., Post.js)

|— routes/        # API routes (e.g., posts.js)

|— controllers/   # Business logic (optional)

|— middleware/    # Middleware functions (optional)

|— .env           # Environment variables

|— index.js       # Entry point

|— package.json   # Project metadata
```

Following this approach ensures our application remains **modular, maintainable, and scalable**.

Conclusion: Laying the Foundation

At this stage, we've successfully set up the core components of our blog application:

- Initialized a **Node.js project** with Express.js.

- Installed essential **dependencies** for backend development.

- Created an **Express.js server** with middleware.

- Established a **MongoDB database connection**.

- Adopted a **structured project layout** for scalability.

With this solid foundation in place, we can now move on to the next step—**designing API endpoints** that will allow us to interact with the blog data. In the upcoming sections, we'll define routes for **creating, retrieving, updating, and deleting blog posts**, making our backend fully functional.

10.2 Designing the API Endpoints

Defining the Heart of Your Backend

Imagine you're building a blogging platform, and you want users to interact with it. They should be able to create blog posts, retrieve them, update content, and delete articles when necessary. But how do we translate these user actions into something our backend can understand? The answer lies in designing a structured set of API endpoints.

API endpoints serve as the bridge between the frontend and the backend. A well-designed API ensures smooth communication, making it easier to scale, secure, and maintain. Poor API design, on the other hand, can lead to confusion, inefficiencies, and security vulnerabilities.

In this chapter, we'll define the core API endpoints for our Express.js blog project. We'll follow **RESTful principles**, ensuring our API is intuitive and follows best practices. We'll also look at potential pitfalls, debugging strategies, and real-world considerations to keep our API efficient and developer-friendly.

Understanding RESTful API Design

Before jumping into the code, it's important to understand the structure of a **RESTful API**.

A RESTful API uses **HTTP methods** to perform actions on **resources**. Each resource (like a blog post) is represented by a **URL**.

Here's a breakdown of common HTTP methods and how they map to CRUD operations:

HTTP Method	Action	Example Endpoint	Description
GET	Read	`/api/posts`	Fetch all blog posts
GET	Read (single item)	`/api/posts/:id`	Fetch a specific blog post
POST	Create	`/api/posts`	Create a new blog post
PUT	Update	`/api/posts/:id`	Update a blog post
DELETE	Delete	`/api/posts/:id`	Delete a blog post

By following this structure, we ensure that our API is predictable and easy to use for frontend developers or other clients consuming it.

Setting Up Routes in Express.js

In our project, we'll keep things organized by separating routes into a dedicated folder. Instead of cluttering our `index.js` file with route definitions, we'll create an `api` directory.

1. Creating the Routes File

Inside your project, create a new folder named `routes` and add a file named `posts.js`.

bash

```
mkdir routes

touch routes/posts.js
```

Open `routes/posts.js` and set up the basic structure:

javascript

```
const express = require("express");

const router = express.Router();

// Placeholder route

router.get("/", (req, res) => {
```

```javascript
    res.send("Blog API is working!");
});
module.exports = router;
```

Now, modify `index.js` to use this routes file:

javascript

```javascript
const express = require("express");
const mongoose = require("mongoose");
const cors = require("cors");
const dotenv = require("dotenv");
const postsRoutes = require("./routes/posts");
dotenv.config();
const app = express();
const PORT = process.env.PORT || 5000;
// Middleware
app.use(express.json());
app.use(cors());

// Routes
```

```
app.use("/api/posts", postsRoutes);


mongoose.connect(process.env.MONGO_URI, {

    useNewUrlParser: true,

    useUnifiedTopology: true,

})

.then(() => console.log("MongoDB connected"))

.catch(err      =>      console.error("Database
connection error:", err));


app.listen(PORT, () => {

    console.log(`Server     running    on    port
${PORT}`);

});
```

Restart your server and visit http://localhost:5000/api/posts. You should see Blog API is working!, confirming that our routing structure is set up correctly.

Building the API Endpoints

Now, let's implement the actual API logic for blog posts. First, we need a **Post model** to interact with MongoDB.

2. Creating the Post Model

Inside a new models directory, create Post.js:

javascript

```javascript
const mongoose = require("mongoose");

const PostSchema = new mongoose.Schema({

    title: { type: String, required: true },

    content: { type: String, required: true },

    author: { type: String, required: true },

    createdAt: { type: Date, default: Date.now
},

});

module.exports = mongoose.model("Post",
PostSchema);
```

This schema defines the structure of a blog post, ensuring each entry has a title, content, author, and a timestamp.

3. Implementing CRUD Routes

Modify   routes/posts.js   to   include   CRUD
functionality.

Fetching All Blog Posts

javascript

```javascript
const express = require("express");

const Post = require("../models/Post");

const router = express.Router();

// Get all posts

router.get("/", async (req, res) => {

    try {

        const posts = await Post.find();

        res.status(200).json(posts);

    } catch (error) {

        res.status(500).json({        message:
"Error retrieving posts", error });

    }

});
```

This route retrieves all blog posts from the database
and returns them as JSON. If an error occurs, we send
a **500 Internal Server Error** response.

Fetching a Single Blog Post

javascript

```javascript
router.get("/:id", async (req, res) => {

    try {

        const post = await
Post.findById(req.params.id);

        if (!post) return
res.status(404).json({ message: "Post not
found" });

        res.status(200).json(post);

    } catch (error) {

        res.status(500).json({ message:
"Error retrieving post", error });

    }

});
```

This endpoint fetches a specific blog post by ID. If the post doesn't exist, we return a **404 Not Found** response.

Creating a New Blog Post

javascript

```javascript
router.post("/", async (req, res) => {
```

```javascript
    try {

        const { title, content, author } =
req.body;

        const newPost = new Post({ title,
content, author });

        await newPost.save();

        res.status(201).json(newPost);

    } catch (error) {

        res.status(500).json({         message:
"Error creating post", error });

    }

});
```

A POST request to `/api/posts` creates a new blog post. The request body must contain `title`, `content`, and `author`.

Updating a Blog Post

javascript

```javascript
router.put("/:id", async (req, res) => {

    try {

        const    updatedPost    =    await
Post.findByIdAndUpdate(req.params.id,
req.body, { new: true });
```

```javascript
        if          (!updatedPost)         return
res.status(404).json({   message:   "Post   not
found" });

        res.status(200).json(updatedPost);

    } catch (error) {

        res.status(500).json({        message:
"Error updating post", error });

    }

});
```

This updates an existing blog post and returns the modified version.

Deleting a Blog Post

javascript

```javascript
router.delete("/:id", async (req, res) => {

    try {

        const     deletedPost     =     await
Post.findByIdAndDelete(req.params.id);

        if          (!deletedPost)         return
res.status(404).json({   message:   "Post   not
found" });

        res.status(200).json({ message: "Post
deleted successfully" });
```

```
    } catch (error) {

        res.status(500).json({        message:
"Error deleting post", error });

    }

});
```

This removes a post from the database and returns a success message.

Conclusion: Designing a Scalable API

At this point, we have successfully built a **RESTful API** with Express.js that supports:

- Retrieving all blog posts

- Fetching a single post by ID

- Creating new blog posts

- Updating existing posts

- Deleting posts

A well-structured API is more than just functional—it's scalable, maintainable, and intuitive. In the next chapter, we'll explore **middleware, authentication, and security**, ensuring our blog API is robust and production-ready.

10.3 Connecting the Frontend with Express.js Backend

Imagine you've built a robust Express.js API that serves dynamic blog posts, user data, and various resources. Now, you need a way to present this data in a user-friendly interface. This is where the frontend comes into play—whether it's built with React, Vue, or Angular, it will consume your API to display dynamic content and offer interactive experiences.

Connecting the frontend to the backend is one of the most critical steps in building a full-stack application. Without proper integration, your application will be a collection of isolated components that cannot communicate effectively. In this chapter, we'll explore how to establish that connection using modern techniques, ensuring seamless data flow, robust error handling, and an overall smooth user experience.

We'll cover:

- **Setting up the frontend environment** (using a modern framework such as React)

- **Making API requests** to your Express.js backend using tools like Axios

- **Handling responses and errors** gracefully in the frontend

- **Best practices** for cross-origin resource sharing (CORS) and secure communication

By the end of this chapter, you'll understand how to integrate your frontend with your Express.js backend, bringing your full-stack application to life.

---

1. Setting Up the Frontend Environment

For this example, we'll use React as our frontend framework. React is widely used, component-based, and works very well with RESTful APIs.

1.1 Creating a New React App

If you haven't already set up a React application, you can quickly bootstrap one using Create React App:

bash

```
npx create-react-app blog-frontend

cd blog-frontend

npm start
```

This command creates a new React project and starts the development server on http://localhost:3000.

1.2 Configuring the Application

Ensure that your Express.js backend is running on a different port (e.g., 5000). You may need to configure your React app to communicate with the backend. This often involves setting up a proxy in the `package.json` file of your React project:

json

```
// Inside blog-frontend/package.json
{
  "proxy": "http://localhost:5000"
}
```

This proxy configuration ensures that API calls from your React app are forwarded to your Express.js backend, eliminating cross-origin issues during development.

---

2. Making API Requests from the Frontend

Once your React environment is ready, the next step is to connect it to the Express.js API. In modern web applications, this is usually done using HTTP clients like Axios or the Fetch API. In our example, we will use Axios.

2.1 Installing Axios

Inside your React project directory, install Axios:

337

bash

```bash
npm install axios
```

2.2 Fetching Data in a React Component

Let's create a simple component that fetches blog posts from the backend. Create a new file `Posts.js` inside the `src` directory:

javascript

```javascript
import React, { useEffect, useState } from "react";

import axios from "axios";

const Posts = () => {

    const [posts, setPosts] = useState([]);

    const [loading, setLoading] = useState(true);

    const [error, setError] = useState("");


    useEffect(() => {

        // Fetch blog posts from the Express backend

        axios.get("/api/posts")

            .then(response => {
```

338

```
              setPosts(response.data);

              setLoading(false);

          })

          .catch(err => {

              console.error("Error  fetching
posts:", err);

              setError("Error        fetching
posts");

              setLoading(false);

          });

  }, []);


  if    (loading)    return    <p>Loading
posts...</p>;

  if (error) return <p>{error}</p>;


  return (

      <div>

          <h1>Blog Posts</h1>

          {posts.length > 0 ? (

              posts.map(post => (
```

```jsx
                    <div key={post._id}>

                        <h2>{post.title}</h2>

                        <p>{post.content}</p>

                        <small>By
{post.author}</small>

                        <hr />

                    </div>

                ))
            ) : (

                <p>No posts available.</p>

            )}

        </div>

    );
};


export default Posts;
```

2.3 Integrating the Component in Your App

Now, update your main `App.js` file to include the `Posts` component:

javascript

```javascript
import React from "react";

import Posts from "./Posts";

function App() {

    return (

        <div className="App">

            <Posts />

        </div>

    );

}

export default App;
```

When you run the React app, it should display a list of blog posts fetched from your Express.js API.

---

3. Handling Responses and Errors

3.1 Graceful Error Handling in the Frontend

While the backend should handle errors gracefully, your frontend must also be prepared to handle failures. In the example above, if the API call fails, an error message is set in state and displayed to the user. This provides a better user experience and helps with debugging.

3.2 Loading States and User Feedback

Providing feedback during API calls is essential. Users should see a loading indicator while data is being fetched. In our example, a simple text message ("Loading posts...") is shown until the data is available.

3.3 Securing API Communication

While developing locally, setting up a proxy helps avoid CORS issues. In production, ensure your Express.js backend is configured to allow requests only from trusted domains using CORS middleware. This protects your API from unauthorized access and ensures secure communication.

---

4. Best Practices for Connecting Frontend and Backend

1. **Keep API URLs Centralized:**
   Store API URLs in a configuration file or environment variables to avoid hardcoding them in multiple components.

2. **Implement Robust Error Handling:**
   Both the backend and frontend should have proper error handling. Display user-friendly error messages and log detailed errors for debugging.

3. **Optimize API Calls:**
   Use pagination, query parameters, and caching strategies on the backend to reduce data load

and improve performance.

4. **Secure Data Transmission:**
   In production, use HTTPS to encrypt data between the frontend and backend. Ensure CORS policies are correctly configured.

5. **Test Thoroughly:**
   Use tools like Postman to test API endpoints and ensure they behave as expected before integrating them into the frontend.

Bringing Your Application to Life

Connecting the frontend with your Express.js backend is the final piece that brings your full-stack application together. Through this chapter, you've learned how to:

- **Set up a modern frontend environment** using React.

- **Configure a proxy** to enable seamless communication between the frontend and backend.

- **Use Axios to fetch data** from your Express.js API.

- **Handle loading states and errors** gracefully to improve user experience.

- **Follow best practices** for security and maintainability.

With these skills, you're well-equipped to create dynamic, data-driven web applications. As you continue developing your projects, remember that a well-connected frontend and backend not only enhance performance but also provide a smoother, more reliable experience for your users.

Next Steps:

- Experiment with state management libraries like Redux or Context API in React for more complex applications.

- Implement authentication on the frontend to secure your API calls.

- Explore advanced optimization techniques such as code splitting and lazy loading for improved performance.

Armed with this knowledge, you're ready to push your full-stack application to the next level, creating robust, production-ready systems that deliver real value to users.

10.4 Implementing CRUD Operations for Blog Posts

Imagine you're building a blog platform. You need to allow users to create posts, update them, delete outdated content, and retrieve posts to display on the frontend. This fundamental functionality—Create, Read, Update, and Delete (CRUD)—forms the backbone of nearly every dynamic web application, from social media platforms to e-commerce stores.

As a backend developer working with Express.js, implementing CRUD operations effectively means ensuring smooth data management, handling errors gracefully, and optimizing database interactions for performance. In this chapter, we'll dive deep into building a blog post API using Express.js and MongoDB (via Mongoose). We'll cover:

- **Setting up the Mongoose model for blog posts**

- **Creating API endpoints for CRUD operations**

- **Handling validation and error scenarios**

- **Optimizing the API for performance and security**

By the end of this chapter, you'll have a solid understanding of how to build a robust API that powers a blog system or any similar content-driven application.

---

1. Setting Up the Blog Post Model

Before implementing CRUD operations, we need a structured way to store blog posts. MongoDB, being a NoSQL database, allows flexible schema design, but using Mongoose helps us define clear models and enforce data consistency.

1.1 Installing Mongoose

Ensure Mongoose is installed in your Express.js project:

bash

```
npm install mongoose
```

1.2 Defining the Blog Post Schema

Create a models directory inside your project and add a new file called Post.js:

javascript

```
const mongoose = require("mongoose");
```

```
const postSchema = new mongoose.Schema(

    {

        title: {

            type: String,

            required:    [true,    "Title    is
required"],

            trim: true,

            maxlength: 100

        },

        content: {

            type: String,

            required: [true, "Content cannot
be empty"]

        },

        author: {

            type: String,

            required: [true, "Author name is
required"]

        },

        createdAt: {
```

```
        type: Date,

        default: Date.now

      }

    },

    { timestamps: true }

);



module.exports    =    mongoose.model("Post",
postSchema);
```

This schema ensures:

- **Required fields** like title, content, and author are always provided.

- **Timestamps** automatically store creation and update times.

- **Trimming and length constraints** help maintain data consistency.

With the model in place, we can now create API routes for CRUD operations.

---

2. Implementing CRUD Routes in Express.js

Now, let's define API routes to interact with the database. Inside your routes directory, create a file called postRoutes.js.

2.1 Creating a New Blog Post (Create)

Users should be able to submit new blog posts through a POST request.

javascript

```javascript
const express = require("express");

const router = express.Router();

const Post = require("../models/Post");


// Create a new post

router.post("/", async (req, res) => {

    try {

        const { title, content, author } =
req.body;


        if (!title || !content || !author) {

            return    res.status(400).json({
error: "All fields are required" });
```

```javascript
    }

    const newPost = new Post({ title,
content, author });

    await newPost.save();


    res.status(201).json(newPost);

  } catch (error) {

    console.error("Error creating post:",
error);

    res.status(500).json({        error:
"Internal Server Error" });

    }

});


module.exports = router;
```

2.2 Retrieving Blog Posts (Read)

Users need to fetch all posts or a specific one.

javascript

```javascript
// Get all posts

router.get("/", async (req, res) => {

    try {

        const posts = await Post.find().sort({
createdAt: -1 });

        res.json(posts);

    } catch (error) {

        console.error("Error          fetching
posts:", error);

        res.status(500).json({ error: "Failed
to retrieve posts" });

    }

});


// Get a single post by ID

router.get("/:id", async (req, res) => {

    try {

        const       post       =       await
Post.findById(req.params.id);

        if          (!post)          return
res.status(404).json({ error: "Post not found"
});
```

```javascript
        res.json(post);

    } catch (error) {

        console.error("Error fetching post:",
error);

        res.status(500).json({ error: "Failed
to retrieve post" });

    }

});
```

2.3 Updating a Blog Post (Update)

Users should be able to edit an existing post.

javascript

```javascript
router.put("/:id", async (req, res) => {

    try {

        const { title, content, author } =
req.body;


        const    updatedPost    =    await
Post.findByIdAndUpdate(
```

```javascript
      req.params.id,

      { title, content, author },

      { new: true, runValidators: true }

    );


    if      (!updatedPost)      return
res.status(404).json({ error: "Post not found"
});


    res.json(updatedPost);

  } catch (error) {

    console.error("Error updating post:",
error);

    res.status(500).json({ error: "Failed
to update post" });

  }
});
```

2.4 Deleting a Blog Post (Delete)

Users should be able to remove posts.

javascript

```javascript
router.delete("/:id", async (req, res) => {

    try {

        const deletedPost = await
Post.findByIdAndDelete(req.params.id);

        if (!deletedPost) return
res.status(404).json({ error: "Post not found"
});


        res.json({ message: "Post deleted
successfully" });

    } catch (error) {

        console.error("Error deleting post:",
error);

        res.status(500).json({ error: "Failed
to delete post" });

    }

});
```

3. Connecting Routes to Express.js

In your main `server.js` or `app.js` file, import and use the blog post routes:

javascript

```javascript
const express = require("express");

const mongoose = require("mongoose");

const cors = require("cors");

const                postRoutes                =
require("./routes/postRoutes");

const app = express();


// Middleware

app.use(express.json());

app.use(cors());

// Database Connection

mongoose.connect("mongodb://localhost:27017/b
log", {

    useNewUrlParser: true,

    useUnifiedTopology: true

})

.then(() => console.log("MongoDB connected"))
```

```
.catch(err       =>       console.error("MongoDB
connection error:", err));


// Routes

app.use("/api/posts", postRoutes);


const PORT = 5000;

app.listen(PORT,   ()   =>   console.log(`Server
running on port ${PORT}`));
```

---

4. Best Practices for CRUD APIs

1. **Validation is crucial** – Use libraries like Joi or built-in validation in Mongoose to prevent bad data from entering your database.

2. **Error handling matters** – Never assume an operation will succeed; always handle errors and provide meaningful messages.

3. **Use proper status codes** – Return the right HTTP status codes (201 for creation, 400 for bad requests, 404 for missing resources, 500 for internal errors).

4. **Implement pagination for large datasets** – Instead of returning all posts, allow clients to request paginated data.

5. **Secure your API** – Protect routes with authentication and authorization, especially when handling sensitive data.

CRUD operations are the foundation of any web application. By implementing them properly in Express.js, you ensure that your backend is well-structured, reliable, and easy to integrate with a frontend.

In this chapter, we built a **fully functional blog post API**, covering:

- Creating, reading, updating, and deleting posts

- Handling validation, error scenarios, and response optimization

- Connecting Express.js to MongoDB and structuring API endpoints efficiently

As a next step, consider adding **authentication and role-based access control (RBAC)** to secure your API, or extend the system with **image uploads and comments** to make your blog more dynamic.

Chapter 11: Deploying Express.js Applications

From Local Development to Global Scale

You've built a great Express.js application, tested it thoroughly, and it's running smoothly on your local machine. But that's only half the battle. The real challenge is making your application accessible to the world, ensuring it runs efficiently under real-world conditions, and handling traffic without crashing.

In the real world, many beginner developers struggle with deployment. You might have written clean code, but the application refuses to start in production. Maybe environment variables aren't loading correctly, or the server crashes after handling just a few requests. Worse, what worked fine on one platform refuses to cooperate on another.

Deploying an Express.js application is more than just copying code to a server. You need to optimize for performance, handle security concerns, and set up a scalable infrastructure that can grow with your user base. In this chapter, we'll go step by step through preparing your Express.js app for production and deploying it on different platforms, including **Heroku, Vercel, and DigitalOcean**. We'll also explore **Docker and Kubernetes** for scalable deployments and **CI/CD pipelines** for automating deployment workflows.

11.1 Preparing an Express.js App for Production

Imagine you've built a fantastic Express.js application. It runs flawlessly on your local machine, and you're excited to share it with the world. But the moment you deploy it, things start going wrong—unexpected crashes, slow responses, security vulnerabilities, and users reporting downtime. What went wrong?

Developing an Express.js app is just half the battle. The real challenge begins when you prepare it for production. Unlike your local environment, where errors are easy to debug and restart, a production system needs to be stable, secure, and performant under real-world traffic.

In this section, we'll cover essential steps to prepare your Express.js app for production, including **environment configuration, error handling, logging, security best practices, and performance optimizations**. These steps ensure that your app not only works but thrives in a production setting.

1. Configuring Environment Variables

Hardcoding sensitive information like database credentials, API keys, or secret tokens in your code is a disaster waiting to happen. If you accidentally push these to a public repository, you risk security breaches and service abuse.

Using dotenv for Secure Configuration

To manage environment variables safely, use the **dotenv** package.

Step 1: Install dotenv

bash

```
npm install dotenv
```

Step 2: Create a .env File

Inside the root of your project, create a `.env` file and store sensitive configurations there.

ini

```
PORT=4000

MONGO_URI=mongodb+srv://your-username:your-password@cluster.mongodb.net/your-db

SECRET_KEY=your-secret-key
```

Step 3: Load Environment Variables in Your Code

Modify your `server.js` file to use dotenv.

javascript

```javascript
require("dotenv").config();

const express = require("express");

const mongoose = require("mongoose");


const app = express();

const PORT = process.env.PORT || 5000;


// Database Connection

mongoose.connect(process.env.MONGO_URI,      {
useNewUrlParser:    true,    useUnifiedTopology:
true })

    .then(()      =>      console.log("Database
connected"))

    .catch(err    =>    console.error("Database
connection error:", err));


app.listen(PORT,   ()   =>   console.log(`Server
running on port ${PORT}`));
```

Why This Matters

- Keeps credentials **out of the source code**.

- Prevents security risks from accidental exposure.

- Makes the application easier to configure across different environments (development, testing, production).

---

2. Implementing Robust Error Handling

A production-ready application must handle errors gracefully. If your app crashes due to an unhandled error, it can take down the entire server. Instead, you want to catch errors early and respond with useful messages.

Centralized Error Handling Middleware

Instead of wrapping every route in `try...catch`, Express allows you to define a **global error handler**.

javascript

```
app.use((err, req, res, next) => {

    console.error("Error:", err.message);

    res.status(500).json({ error: "Something
went wrong, please try again later." });

});
```

Now, if an error occurs anywhere in your routes, Express will automatically pass it to this middleware.

Handling Uncaught Exceptions and Rejections

To prevent your app from crashing due to unhandled errors, listen for these global exceptions:

javascript

```javascript
process.on("uncaughtException", (err) => {

    console.error("Uncaught        Exception:",
err);

    process.exit(1);

});




process.on("unhandledRejection",        (reason,
promise) => {

    console.error("Unhandled        Rejection:",
reason);

});
```

Why This Matters

- Prevents the server from crashing due to unexpected errors.

- Logs errors for debugging instead of exposing raw messages to users.

- Improves user experience by providing clear, actionable error responses.

---

3. Logging and Monitoring

You can't fix what you don't measure. Logging is critical in production to diagnose issues, monitor traffic, and detect anomalies.

Using Winston for Logging

Winston is a popular logging library that helps track application events and errors.

Step 1: Install Winston

bash

```
npm install winston
```

Step 2: Create a Logger

javascript

```
const winston = require("winston");
```

```
const logger = winston.createLogger({

    level: "info",

    format: winston.format.json(),

    transports: [

        new             winston.transports.File({
filename: "error.log", level: "error" }),

        new             winston.transports.Console({
format: winston.format.simple() }),

    ],

});


logger.info("Application                    started
successfully");
```

Now, whenever an error occurs, it will be logged instead of being lost.

Why This Matters

- Helps **debug production issues** without direct server access.

- Logs **critical errors and warnings** to investigate problems later.

- Improves **observability**, making maintenance easier.

---

4. Security Best Practices

A production Express.js app must be secure. Attackers often target misconfigured applications, and a single vulnerability can compromise an entire system.

Essential Security Enhancements

1. Helmet for Securing HTTP Headers

Helmet helps set secure HTTP headers to prevent common web vulnerabilities.

bash

```
npm install helmet
```

javascript

```
const helmet = require("helmet");
app.use(helmet());
```

2. Rate Limiting to Prevent Abuse

To prevent brute-force attacks, limit the number of requests a user can make.

bash

```
npm install express-rate-limit
```

javascript

```
const rateLimit = require("express-rate-limit");

const limiter = rateLimit({
    windowMs: 15 * 60 * 1000, // 15 minutes
    max: 100, // Limit each IP to 100 requests per windowMs
    message: "Too many requests, please try again later.",
});
```

```
app.use(limiter);
```

3. CORS for Secure API Access

Enable **Cross-Origin Resource Sharing (CORS)** for API security.

bash

```
npm install cors
```

javascript

```
const cors = require("cors");
app.use(cors());
```

Why This Matters

- Prevents **cross-site scripting (XSS)** and **clickjacking** attacks.

- Reduces **brute-force login attempts** with rate limiting.

- Controls **who can access your API**, reducing security risks.

5. Using a Process Manager

In production, your app shouldn't go down because of a crash. A **process manager** keeps it running and restarts it if it fails.

Using PM2

PM2 is a powerful process manager for Node.js applications.

Step 1: Install PM2

bash

```
npm install pm2 -g
```

Step 2: Start Your App

bash

```
pm2 start server.js --name "express-app"
```

Step 3: Ensure the App Runs on Reboots

bash

```
pm2 save

pm2 startup
```

Why This Matters

- Keeps the app running **even if it crashes**.

- Automatically **restarts the app** when the server reboots.

- Provides **logs and monitoring** for better debugging.

Conclusion: Preparing for Production Success

A production-ready Express.js application is more than just code—it's **optimized for security, stability, and performance**.

- **Environment variables** keep sensitive data safe.

- **Error handling** ensures graceful failures instead of crashes.

- **Logging** helps diagnose issues in real-world scenarios.

- **Security best practices** protect against common attacks.

- **Process management** keeps the app running with minimal downtime.

With these strategies, your Express.js app is ready to handle **real users, real traffic, and real challenges**.

11.2 Deploying on Heroku, Vercel, and DigitalOcean

You've built an Express.js application that runs flawlessly on your local machine. Everything is smooth—your APIs respond quickly, the database is connected, and debugging is simple. But now, you need to take it live. How do you get your app on the internet, accessible to real users?

Deployment is one of the most critical steps in the development process. A well-deployed application is reliable, scalable, and easy to maintain. A poorly deployed one? Frequent downtime, security vulnerabilities, and sluggish performance.

Choosing the right platform for deployment depends on your needs. Some developers want a **quick and easy** way to deploy an Express.js app without managing infrastructure. Others need **flexibility and control** over their server environment. In this chapter, we'll explore three popular deployment platforms— **Heroku, Vercel, and DigitalOcean**—each offering different levels of simplicity and control.

By the end, you'll have a clear understanding of how to deploy your Express.js application to each platform, along with best practices for keeping it running smoothly.

---

1. Deploying on Heroku

Heroku is a **developer-friendly, platform-as-a-service (PaaS)** that simplifies deployment. It abstracts infrastructure management, making it ideal for beginners.

Step 1: Install the Heroku CLI

To deploy your app, first, install the Heroku CLI:

Mac/Linux (via Homebrew):

bash

```
brew install heroku
```

- **Windows**: Download and install from Heroku CLI.

Once installed, log in:

bash

```
heroku login
```

Step 2: Prepare Your App

Ensure your project has a `package.json` with a start script:

json

```json
"scripts": {
  "start": "node server.js"
}
```

And create a **Procfile** in the root directory:

makefile

```makefile
web: node server.js
```

Step 3: Initialize a Git Repository and Deploy

bash

```bash
git init
heroku create your-app-name
git add .
git commit -m "Initial deployment"
git push heroku master
```

Your app is now live. Run:

bash

```
heroku open
```

Common Pitfalls

Port Issues: Heroku assigns a dynamic port, so update your `server.js`:

javascript

```javascript
const PORT = process.env.PORT || 5000;

app.listen(PORT, () => console.log(`Server running on port ${PORT}`));
```

Environment Variables: Set them using:

bash
```bash
heroku config:set MONGO_URI=your-database-url
```

Why Use Heroku?

- **Easy setup** for beginners.

- **Free tier available** for small projects.

- **Built-in scaling** for handling traffic.

2. Deploying on Vercel

Vercel is **optimized for frontend applications**, but it also supports backend services, including Express.js. It's known for its **serverless deployment model**, meaning your API runs as **functions** that scale automatically.

Step 1: Install the Vercel CLI

bash

```
npm install -g vercel

vercel login
```

Step 2: Prepare Your Express.js App

Modify your `server.js` to use `vercel.json`:

javascript

```
const express = require("express");

const app = express();


app.get("/", (req, res) => res.send("Hello from Vercel!"));


module.exports = app;
```

Create a **vercel.json** file to configure the deployment:

json

```json
{
  "version": 2,
  "builds": [{ "src": "server.js", "use": "@vercel/node" }],
  "routes": [{ "src": "/(.*)", "dest": "/server.js" }]
}
```

Step 3: Deploy Your App

bash

```bash
vercel
```

Common Pitfalls

- **Cold Start Delays**: Since Vercel runs Express.js as a **serverless function**, the first request may be slightly slower if the function is inactive.

- **File System Restrictions**: Unlike traditional servers, serverless environments **do not**

persist files, so avoid writing to disk.

Why Use Vercel?

- **Perfect for serverless applications**.

- **Auto-scaling with no manual setup**.

- **Quick deployments with minimal configuration**.

---

3. Deploying on DigitalOcean

For developers who need **more control** over their infrastructure, DigitalOcean provides **Virtual Private Servers (VPS)** where you have full root access.

Step 1: Create a Droplet

1. Sign up at DigitalOcean.

2. Create a **Droplet** using the **Ubuntu image**.

3. Choose a basic plan (the $4/month plan is sufficient for small applications).

Once the Droplet is created, SSH into it:

bash

```
ssh root@your-server-ip
```

Step 2: Install Node.js and Express

bash

```
curl                              -fsSL
https://deb.nodesource.com/setup_18.x | bash -
apt-get install -y nodejs
```

Verify installation:

bash

```
node -v
```

Step 3: Deploy Your Express.js App

Clone   your   repository:

bash

```
git clone https://github.com/your-repo.git
cd your-repo
```

Install dependencies:

bash
```
npm install
```

Start the application with **PM2**:

bash
```bash
npm install -g pm2

pm2 start server.js --name express-app

pm2 startup

pm2 save
```

Set up **NGINX as a reverse proxy** (optional but recommended):

bash
```bash
apt install nginx

nano /etc/nginx/sites-available/default
```

Add the following configuration:

nginx
```nginx
server {
    listen 80;
    server_name your-domain.com;

    location / {
        proxy_pass http://localhost:5000;
```

379

```
        proxy_set_header Host $host;

        proxy_set_header            X-Real-IP
$remote_addr;

    }

}
```

1.

Restart   NGINX:

bash

```
systemctl restart nginx
```

2.

Common Pitfalls

Firewall Issues: Ensure your firewall allows
HTTP/HTTPS   traffic:

bash

```
ufw allow 80

ufw allow 443

ufw enable
```

-
  - **Process Management**: Without PM2, your app
    won't restart if the server reboots.

Why Use DigitalOcean?

- **Full control over the server**.

- **Ideal for production-grade apps**.

- **More flexibility compared to PaaS providers like Heroku and Vercel**.

Each deployment method serves different use cases:

- **Heroku**: Great for beginners who want fast, easy deployment without managing infrastructure.

- **Vercel**: Ideal for serverless Express.js apps, perfect for APIs that scale dynamically.

- **DigitalOcean**: The best choice for developers who need full control over their server environment.

The best platform depends on your project's requirements. If you're building a simple API, **Heroku or Vercel** might be enough. If you need full control over your stack, **DigitalOcean** is the way to go.

With your app now deployed, the next step is **optimizing performance and security in a real-world environment**, ensuring it can handle traffic, scale efficiently, and remain secure.

11.3 Using Docker and Kubernetes for Scalable Deployment

Deploying an Express.js application is one thing. Ensuring it runs **smoothly** under increasing traffic is another challenge entirely. If you've ever had an application **crash** because too many users accessed it at once, or struggled with **inconsistent environments** between development and production, you're not alone.

Scalability is a crucial factor in modern web applications. As your user base grows, your infrastructure must adapt. Running your application manually on a single server works for small projects, but **what happens when you need to handle thousands of requests per second?**

This is where **Docker** and **Kubernetes** come in. Docker helps **containerize** applications, making deployments more consistent and manageable. Kubernetes takes it a step further by **orchestrating** these containers, ensuring your app runs efficiently across multiple machines.

By the end of this chapter, you'll understand:

- How **Docker** simplifies deployment by packaging your Express.js app into a container

- How **Kubernetes** manages multiple containers for high availability and scalability

- How to deploy your containerized Express.js app in a production-ready environment

---

1. Understanding Docker: Why It Matters

Imagine you develop an Express.js app on your local machine. It works perfectly. But when you deploy it on a cloud server, suddenly **it throws errors** because of differences in dependencies, OS, or environment variables.

Docker eliminates this problem by packaging your application **and its entire environment** into a standardized unit called a **container**. This means:

- Your app will run **exactly the same way** on any machine, whether it's your laptop, a test server, or production.

- You don't have to worry about **dependency mismatches** or "works on my machine" issues.

1.1 Creating a Dockerfile for Express.js

A **Dockerfile** is a blueprint that tells Docker how to build your container. Let's create one for a simple Express.js app.

Dockerfile

dockerfile

```
# Use an official Node.js image as the base
FROM node:18


# Set the working directory inside the
container
WORKDIR /app


# Copy package.json and package-lock.json
COPY package*.json ./


# Install dependencies
RUN npm install


# Copy the rest of the application files
COPY . .


# Expose port 5000 for the Express app
EXPOSE 5000


# Start the application
```

```
CMD ["node", "server.js"]
```

1.2 Building and Running the Docker Container

Build   the   Docker   image:

bash

```
docker build -t my-express-app .
```

Run   the   container:

bash

```
docker run -p 5000:5000 my-express-app
```

1. **Check your app:** Open
   `http://localhost:5000` in your browser.

At this point, your Express.js app is running **inside a container**, isolated from the host system.

---

2. Docker Compose: Running Multiple Services

Most real-world apps need more than just Express.js. You might need a **database** or a **cache service**. Instead of running everything manually, **Docker**

Compose allows you to define and manage multiple containers effortlessly.

2.1 Writing a Docker Compose File

Create a `docker-compose.yml` file:

yaml

```yaml
version: '3.8'

services:
  app:
    build: .
    ports:
      - "5000:5000"
    environment:
      - NODE_ENV=production
    depends_on:
      - db

  db:
    image: mongo:latest
```

```
    container_name: mongodb

    ports:

        - "27017:27017"
```

2.2 Running the Multi-Container App

Start both containers with:

bash

```
docker-compose up -d
```

Your Express.js app and MongoDB instance are now running in **separate, but connected containers**, making deployments cleaner and more scalable.

---

3. Scaling with Kubernetes

Docker containers are great, but manually managing multiple containers across different machines can be overwhelming. Kubernetes (K8s) solves this by **automating deployment, scaling, and management** of containerized applications.

3.1 Key Kubernetes Concepts

Before jumping in, let's break down some **essential Kubernetes components**:

- **Pods**: The smallest deployable unit in Kubernetes, usually running a single container.

- **Deployments**: Manages and scales multiple replicas of a Pod.

- **Services**: Exposes your application to the network, allowing communication between Pods.

3.2 Writing a Kubernetes Deployment for Express.js

Create a Kubernetes deployment file (deployment.yaml):

yaml

```yaml
apiVersion: apps/v1

kind: Deployment

metadata:

  name: express-app

spec:

  replicas: 3

  selector:

    matchLabels:
```

```yaml
      app: express-app

  template:

    metadata:

      labels:

        app: express-app

    spec:

      containers:

        - name: express-container

          image: my-express-app:latest

          ports:

            - containerPort: 5000
```

This defines an **Express.js deployment with three replicas**, meaning Kubernetes will run **three identical instances** of your app for scalability and redundancy.

3.3 Creating a Service to Expose the App

Kubernetes uses **services** to expose apps inside or outside the cluster.

Create service.yaml:

yaml

389

```
apiVersion: v1

kind: Service

metadata:

  name: express-service

spec:

  selector:

    app: express-app

  ports:

    - protocol: TCP

      port: 80

      targetPort: 5000

  type: LoadBalancer
```

Now your app will be accessible on port 80, automatically load-balancing traffic across multiple replicas.

3.4 Deploying on Kubernetes

Apply the deployment:

bash

```
kubectl apply -f deployment.yaml
```

Apply the service:

bash

```
kubectl apply -f service.yaml
```

Check running pods:

bash

```
kubectl get pods
```

Get service URL:

bash

```
kubectl get services
```

   1.

Your Express.js app is now running on a **self-healing, scalable infrastructure**.

11.4 CI/CD Pipelines for Automated Deployment

Imagine this: You've just pushed a new feature to your Express.js application, and now it's time to deploy it. You log into your server, pull the latest code, install dependencies, restart the app, and hope nothing breaks. It works—this time.

But what happens when your team grows? Or when you need to deploy multiple times a day? **Manually deploying changes becomes a nightmare.** There's always a risk of missing a step, forgetting to restart the server, or accidentally overwriting the wrong environment variable.

This is why modern development teams rely on **Continuous Integration (CI) and Continuous Deployment (CD) pipelines**. With CI/CD, your application is automatically **tested, built, and deployed** every time you push code, ensuring consistency and reducing human error.

By the end of this chapter, you'll understand:

- How CI/CD pipelines streamline deployment

- How to set up a GitHub Actions pipeline for an Express.js app

- How to deploy an application to a cloud provider like **AWS, DigitalOcean, or Heroku**

- Best practices for making CI/CD reliable and efficient

---

1. What is CI/CD and Why Does It Matter?

CI/CD is all about **automation**. Let's break it down:

- **Continuous Integration (CI)**: Every time a developer pushes code, the system automatically **runs tests** and **builds** the application to catch errors early.

- **Continuous Deployment (CD)**: If everything passes, the system **automatically deploys** the new version to production.

This means you can release updates **faster and with fewer errors**, making your development workflow more efficient.

1.1 The Real-World Benefits of CI/CD

- **No More "It Works on My Machine"**: Your app runs in a **consistent environment** across all stages.

- **Faster Feedback Loops**: Bugs are detected early, preventing major issues later.

- **Less Manual Work**: Developers can focus on writing code instead of managing deployments.

---

2. Setting Up a CI/CD Pipeline with GitHub Actions

2.1 Why GitHub Actions?

GitHub Actions is a powerful CI/CD tool that integrates **directly with your GitHub repository**. It allows you to automate workflows **without needing additional tools** like Jenkins or Travis CI.

We'll create a **GitHub Actions workflow** that:

1. Runs tests on every push

2. Builds the application

3. Deploys it to a cloud provider (e.g., **AWS, DigitalOcean, or Heroku**)

2.2 Writing a GitHub Actions Workflow for Express.js

Inside your repository, create a `.github/workflows/deploy.yml` file:

yaml

```yaml
name: CI/CD Pipeline

on:
  push:
    branches:
      - main

jobs:
  build-and-test:
    runs-on: ubuntu-latest

    steps:
      - name: Checkout repository
        uses: actions/checkout@v3

      - name: Set up Node.js
        uses: actions/setup-node@v3
        with:
          node-version: 18
```

```yaml
    - name: Install dependencies

      run: npm install


    - name: Run tests

      run: npm test


  deploy:

    needs: build-and-test

    runs-on: ubuntu-latest


    steps:

      - name: Deploy to Production

        run: |

          ssh user@your-server 'cd /path-to-
app && git pull && npm install && pm2 restart
all'

        env:

          SSH_KEY: ${{ secrets.SSH_KEY }}
```

2.3 How This Workflow Works

- **Step 1: Runs tests on each push to** `main`

- **Step 2: If tests pass, pulls the latest code on the server and restarts the application**

This simple pipeline ensures **your application is tested and deployed automatically**, reducing manual intervention.

---

3. Deploying to a Cloud Provider

3.1 Deploying to DigitalOcean with GitHub Actions

If you're using a **VPS** like DigitalOcean, deployment involves **pulling code, installing dependencies, and restarting the app**.

1. Add your server's **SSH key** as a **GitHub Secret** (`SSH_KEY`).

2. Modify the `deploy` job in your workflow:

yaml

```yaml
deploy:

  needs: build-and-test

  runs-on: ubuntu-latest
```

```yaml
steps:

  - name: Deploy to DigitalOcean

    run: |

      ssh -i $SSH_KEY user@your-server 'cd
/app && git pull && npm install && pm2 restart
server'
```

3.2 Deploying to Heroku

Heroku simplifies deployment with a **Git-based workflow**. To automate deployments:

Install the **Heroku CLI**:

bash

```bash
npm install -g heroku
```

Authenticate with Heroku:

bash

```bash
heroku login
```

1. Add Heroku to your **GitHub Actions workflow**:

yaml

```
deploy:

  needs: build-and-test

  runs-on: ubuntu-latest


  steps:

    - name: Deploy to Heroku

      run: |

        heroku git:remote -a your-heroku-app

        git push heroku main

      env:

        HEROKU_API_KEY:                    ${{
secrets.HEROKU_API_KEY }}
```

Every time you push to main, GitHub Actions will **deploy your app to Heroku automatically**.

---

4. Best Practices for CI/CD Pipelines

4.1 Keep Your Pipelines Fast

- Cache dependencies to **reduce build times**

- Run tests **in parallel**

- Only trigger deployments on changes to `main`

4.2 Secure Your Pipeline

- **Never hardcode credentials**—use **GitHub Secrets**

- Restrict deployments to **authorized branches**

4.3 Monitor and Rollback Deployments

- Set up **error monitoring** (e.g., **Sentry, Datadog**)

- Use **blue-green deployments** to minimize downtime

Why CI/CD is a Game-Changer

CI/CD pipelines remove **manual deployment headaches**, ensuring your Express.js app is always **tested, secure, and up to date**.

- **Continuous Integration** catches bugs **before they reach production**

- **Continuous Deployment** automates releases, saving developers time

- Using **GitHub Actions, DigitalOcean, or Heroku**, you can deploy code **within seconds**

If you're serious about building **scalable** applications, **CI/CD is not optional—it's a necessity**.

The next step? Integrating **automated security scans** and **performance monitoring** into your pipeline to further improve deployment reliability.

Chapter 12: Performance Optimization and Security Best Practices

Your Express.js app is live. It works. Users are signing up, browsing, and making API requests. But then, strange things start happening. The app slows down under increased traffic. You notice that some users are being redirected to phishing sites. Your database gets flooded with malicious requests, slowing everything to a crawl.

These aren't just theoretical problems—they happen **all the time** in real-world applications. **Performance issues drive users away. Security vulnerabilities destroy trust.** If your Express.js app isn't optimized for speed and security, it's only a matter of time before something goes wrong.

In this chapter, we'll tackle **two critical areas**:

1. **Improving Express.js performance** to handle more traffic efficiently.

2. **Securing your application** against common attacks like XSS, CSRF, and SQL injection.

By the end of this chapter, you'll not only understand **what** to optimize and secure—you'll also know **how** and **why** each technique matters.

12.1 Improving Express.js Performance

Picture this: You've built a solid Express.js application. Everything works as expected—until traffic spikes. Suddenly, API response times slow down, the server struggles under the load, and users start dropping off. Even worse, you check the logs and see a flood of unnecessary database queries and bloated request payloads slowing things down.

This is the reality of web applications in production. Without proper optimization, an Express.js server can become a bottleneck, frustrating users and limiting scalability. The good news? A few **strategic improvements** can make your application significantly faster, more efficient, and ready to handle real-world demand.

In this section, we'll explore **practical performance optimization techniques** that every Express.js developer should know, from middleware efficiency to caching and database optimizations.

---

1. Optimize Middleware Usage

Middleware is a core feature of Express.js, allowing you to handle requests, parse data, and enforce security policies. However, inefficient middleware can **drastically slow down** your app, especially if unnecessary processing happens on every request.

Use Middleware Selectively

A common mistake is applying middleware **globally**, even when it's only needed for specific routes. For example, `express.json()` is often applied to all routes, even though only a few might need to parse JSON.

Instead of this:

javascript

```javascript
const express = require('express');

const app = express();

app.use(express.json()); // Applied to all routes

app.post('/submit', (req, res) => {

  res.send(`Received:
${JSON.stringify(req.body)}`);

});

app.get('/data', (req, res) => {

  res.send('No JSON parsing needed here.');

});
```

Do this:

javascript

```javascript
app.post('/submit', express.json(), (req, res)
=> {
```

```
    res.send(`Received:
${JSON.stringify(req.body)}`);

});
```

Now, the `express.json()` middleware runs **only when necessary**, reducing overhead on routes that don't need it.

Remove Unused Middleware

If your application has grown over time, you might have middleware that **is no longer needed**. Audit your middleware stack and remove anything redundant.

To check middleware execution order, use:

javascript

```
app._router.stack.forEach((layer) => {

  if (layer.route) {

    console.log(layer.route.path);

  }

});
```

2. Implement Response Compression

By default, Express.js sends responses **without compression**, which wastes bandwidth and slows down client-side rendering. To improve this, use the compression middleware.

javascript

```javascript
const compression = require('compression');

app.use(compression());
```

This significantly reduces response sizes, making your API faster for clients, especially those on slow connections.

---

3. Use Caching to Reduce Unnecessary Computation

Every time a request hits your server, Express runs logic to process it. If the same request is made **multiple times**, recalculating results each time is inefficient.

In-Memory Caching with Redis

Redis is a great tool for storing frequently used data, reducing the need for repeated database queries.

javascript

```javascript
const redis = require('redis');

const client = redis.createClient();

app.get('/data', async (req, res) => {
```

```
client.get('cachedData', async (err, data)
=> {

    if (data) {

        return res.json(JSON.parse(data)); //
Serve from cache

    }

    const        freshData        =        await
fetchDataFromDatabase();      //      Expensive
operation

    client.setex('cachedData',              3600,
JSON.stringify(freshData)); // Cache for 1
hour

    res.json(freshData);

  });

});
```

This ensures that frequently requested data is served **instantly** instead of making expensive database calls each time.

---

4. Optimize Database Queries

Express.js applications often become **sluggish due to inefficient database interactions**. The way you query your database can make a huge difference in performance.

Use Indexes for Faster Queries

If your database queries are slow, check if your tables have **indexes** on frequently queried columns.

For example, in MySQL:

sql

```
CREATE INDEX idx_users_email ON users(email);
```

This speeds up lookups by avoiding full table scans.

Use Connection Pooling

If your app makes frequent database connections, a connection pool can **reuse existing connections**, reducing the overhead of establishing new ones.

Example using MySQL in Node.js:

javascript

```
const mysql = require('mysql2/promise');

const pool = mysql.createPool({

  host: 'localhost',

  user: 'root',

  password: 'password',

  database: 'mydb',

  connectionLimit: 10, // Limit concurrent connections
```

```javascript
});

app.get('/users', async (req, res) => {

  const [rows] = await pool.query('SELECT *
FROM users');

  res.json(rows);

});
```

5. Reduce Payload Size for API Responses

Sending **large payloads** over the network slows down
responses and increases latency.

Use Pagination for Large Data Sets

Instead of returning **all results** in one response,
paginate the data.

Example: Implementing pagination in an API
response.

javascript

```javascript
app.get('/products', async (req, res) => {

  const page = parseInt(req.query.page) || 1;

  const limit = 10;

  const offset = (page - 1) * limit;
```

```javascript
const [products] = await db.query(
  'SELECT * FROM products LIMIT ? OFFSET ?',
  [limit, offset]
);
res.json({ page, products });
});
```

Now, the API returns **only 10 items at a time**, reducing payload size and improving response speed.

---

6. Optimize Static Asset Delivery

If your Express.js app serves static files (images, CSS, JavaScript), consider optimizing how they are delivered.

Use a CDN (Content Delivery Network)

Instead of serving static assets directly from your Express server, use a CDN like **Cloudflare or AWS CloudFront** to distribute them globally.

If you must serve static files from Express, use `express.static()` with caching:

javascript

```javascript
app.use(express.static('public', { maxAge: '1d' })); // Cache files for 1 day
```

7. Implement a Reverse Proxy (Nginx) for Load Balancing

As your traffic grows, a single Express.js instance won't be enough. A **reverse proxy** like Nginx can distribute traffic across multiple instances of your app.

A simple Nginx configuration to load balance requests:

nginx

```
server {

    listen 80;

    location / {

        proxy_pass http://localhost:3000;

        proxy_set_header Host $host;

        proxy_set_header          X-Real-IP
$remote_addr;

    }

}
```

This setup allows you to **run multiple Express instances** behind Nginx, improving scalability.

Performance optimization isn't just about speed—it's about **scalability, efficiency, and user experience**. In this section, we explored several key techniques:

411

- **Middleware optimization**: Use only what's necessary to avoid unnecessary processing.

- **Response compression**: Reduce payload sizes for faster delivery.

- **Caching with Redis**: Store frequently requested data to reduce database load.

- **Database optimizations**: Use indexing, connection pooling, and pagination.

- **Reducing response payloads**: Avoid sending excessive data.

- **CDNs and static asset caching**: Improve static file delivery.

- **Reverse proxy with Nginx**: Load balance requests across multiple instances.

With these strategies in place, your Express.js application will be **faster, more scalable, and ready to handle real-world traffic.**

As a next step, consider **profiling your application's performance** using tools like **New Relic, Datadog, or the built-in Node.js Performance API**. Understanding where bottlenecks occur will help you refine and improve performance even further.

12.2 Preventing Common Security Vulnerabilities (XSS, CSRF, SQL Injection)

Imagine this: You've spent months building your Express.js application. It's feature-rich, the UI looks polished, and everything seems to be working smoothly. Then, one day, you wake up to find that your database has been wiped, user passwords are leaked, and your server is flooded with malicious requests.

What went wrong?

Most likely, your application had one or more security vulnerabilities that an attacker exploited. The unfortunate reality is that web applications are **prime targets for cyberattacks**. Whether it's SQL injection, cross-site scripting (XSS), or data leaks due to misconfigured headers, even a small oversight can lead to devastating consequences.

But here's the good news: **you can prevent most security vulnerabilities with proper precautions**. In this chapter, we'll walk through the most common security threats in Express.js applications and how to defend against them with practical, real-world strategies.

413

1. Protecting Against SQL Injection

The Threat

SQL injection (SQLi) occurs when an attacker manipulates an application's database query by injecting malicious SQL statements. This can allow them to read, modify, or even delete database records.

Consider an Express route that retrieves user data based on an email parameter:

javascript

```javascript
app.get('/user', async (req, res) => {

  const email = req.query.email;

  const user = await db.query(`SELECT * FROM users WHERE email = '${email}'`);

  res.json(user);

});
```

Now, imagine an attacker sends this request:

sql

```sql
GET /user?email=' OR '1'='1
```

Since `1=1` is always true, this query returns **all users in the database**. Worse, if the attacker modifies the input further, they might **delete all records** with something like:

414

sql

```
GET /user?email='; DROP TABLE users; --
```

The Fix: Use Parameterized Queries

The safest way to prevent SQL injection is to use **prepared statements** or **query parameterization**, which ensures user inputs are treated as data, not executable code.

If using MySQL with `mysql2` in Node.js, rewrite the query like this:

javascript

```
const [user] = await db.execute('SELECT * FROM users WHERE email = ?', [email]);
```

For PostgreSQL with `pg`:

javascript

```
const user = await pool.query('SELECT * FROM users WHERE email = $1', [email]);
```

By using placeholders (`?` or `$1`), the database treats user input as **a value** rather than part of the SQL statement, preventing injection attacks.

---

2. Preventing Cross-Site Scripting (XSS)

The Threat

XSS attacks occur when an attacker injects malicious JavaScript into a web page. If the application doesn't properly sanitize user input, this JavaScript can execute in another user's browser—stealing cookies, modifying content, or redirecting users to malicious sites.

A vulnerable Express.js route that renders user input might look like this:

javascript

```
app.get('/search', (req, res) => {

  const query = req.query.q;

  res.send(`<h1>Search        Results        for
${query}</h1>`);

});
```

If a user visits this URL:

416

php-template

```
http://yourapp.com/search?q=<script>alert('Ha
cked!')</script>
```

The browser **executes** the injected script, which could be used to steal cookies or deface the site.

The Fix: Escape User Input and Use Content Security Policies

To prevent XSS, always **sanitize user input** before displaying it in HTML. A popular library for escaping user input is `sanitize-html`:

javascript

```javascript
const sanitizeHtml = require('sanitize-html');

app.get('/search', (req, res) => {

  const query = sanitizeHtml(req.query.q);

  res.send(`<h1>Search        Results        for
${query}</h1>`);

});
```

Additionally, **set a strong Content Security Policy (CSP)** to block inline scripts and only allow JavaScript from trusted sources:

javascript

```javascript
const helmet = require('helmet');

app.use(

  helmet.contentSecurityPolicy({

    directives: {

      defaultSrc: ["'self'"],

      scriptSrc:      ["'self'",      'trusted-
cdn.com'],

    },

  })

);
```

---

3. Securing API Endpoints with Authentication & Rate Limiting

The Threat

Without proper authentication and rate limiting, your API endpoints are vulnerable to:

- **Unauthorized access**: Attackers gaining access to sensitive data.

- **Brute-force attacks**: Repeated login attempts until a password is guessed.

- **Denial of Service (DoS)**: Overloading the server with too many requests.

The Fix: Use JWTs, API Keys, and Rate Limiting

Implement JWT authentication for protected routes:

javascript

```javascript
const jwt = require('jsonwebtoken');

app.post('/login', (req, res) => {

  const user = { id: 1, username:
req.body.username }; // Example user

  const token = jwt.sign(user,
process.env.JWT_SECRET, { expiresIn: '1h' });

  res.json({ token });

});
```

Protect sensitive routes using express-jwt:

javascript

```javascript
const { expressjwt: jwtMiddleware } =
require('express-jwt');
```

```javascript
app.use('/protected', jwtMiddleware({ secret:
process.env.JWT_SECRET, algorithms: ['HS256']
}));
```

Implement rate limiting to prevent abuse using
express-rate-limit:

javascript

```javascript
const    rateLimit    =    require('express-rate-
limit');

const limiter = rateLimit({

  windowMs: 15 * 60 * 1000, // 15 minutes

  max: 100, // Limit each IP to 100 requests
per window

});

app.use('/api/', limiter);
```

4. Preventing Cross-Site Request Forgery (CSRF)

The Threat

CSRF attacks trick a user into **unknowingly
submitting a request** to a web app where they're
authenticated. This can lead to actions like

transferring funds, changing passwords, or deleting accounts.

The Fix: Use CSRF Tokens

Use csurf to generate and verify CSRF tokens for sensitive requests:

javascript

```
const csrf = require('csurf');

const csrfProtection = csrf({ cookie: true });


app.use(csrfProtection);


app.get('/form', (req, res) => {

  res.send(`<form             action="/submit"
method="POST">

             <input               type="hidden"
name="_csrf" value="${req.csrfToken()}">

             <button
type="submit">Submit</button>

          </form>`);

});
```

This ensures that **only legitimate forms generated by your server** can submit data.

Security is **not an afterthought**—it's a fundamental part of building a web application. In this chapter, we covered:

- **SQL injection protection** using parameterized queries.

- **XSS prevention** with input sanitization and Content Security Policies.

- **API security** using JWT authentication and rate limiting.

- **CSRF protection** with tokens to prevent unauthorized actions.

Every Express.js application, no matter how small, should implement these security measures. **Even a single vulnerability can be costly**—so make security a habit in your development process.

As a next step, explore security-focused libraries like `helmet`, monitor vulnerabilities with `npm audit`, and stay updated with the latest security best practices. Security is an ongoing process, and by integrating these principles early, you'll build safer and more resilient applications.

12.3 Implementing Rate Limiting, CORS, and Helmet for Secure Applications

Imagine launching your Express.js API, only to see it **slow down, crash, or get bombarded with suspicious requests** within days. Some requests seem normal, but others flood your server at an alarming rate. Meanwhile, you start receiving security warnings about potential **CORS misconfigurations** and **missing security headers** that make your app an easy target.

What went wrong?

The reality is that modern web applications **face constant threats**—from malicious bots attempting to overload your server to browsers enforcing strict cross-origin policies that break functionality. **Without the right safeguards, your Express app is vulnerable.**

In this chapter, we'll explore three critical protections every Express.js application should have:

- **Rate limiting** to prevent abuse and denial-of-service (DoS) attacks.

- **Cross-Origin Resource Sharing (CORS)** to control how your API interacts with different domains.

- **Helmet** to enforce security best practices with HTTP headers.

By the end of this chapter, you'll have a **robust, production-ready** Express setup that can handle traffic efficiently while staying secure.

---

1. Implementing Rate Limiting in Express

The Threat: Uncontrolled API Requests

Let's say you have a login endpoint:

javascript

```
app.post('/login', (req, res) => {

  // Authenticate user

});
```

What happens if an attacker writes a simple script that sends **thousands of login attempts per second**?

- Your server resources get exhausted.

- It opens the door for **brute-force attacks** on user accounts.

- Legitimate users start experiencing slow responses—or worse, downtime.

The Fix: Use Express Rate Limiting

Rate limiting **controls how often a client (IP address) can make requests** within a specific time window. In Express.js, the `express-rate-limit` middleware is the simplest way to implement this.

Installing express-rate-limit

First, install the package:

sh

```
npm install express-rate-limit
```

Now, apply it to your API:

javascript

```javascript
const rateLimit = require('express-rate-limit');

const limiter = rateLimit({

  windowMs: 15 * 60 * 1000, // 15 minutes

  max: 100, // Limit each IP to 100 requests per window

  message: 'Too many requests, please try again later.',

  headers: true,

});

app.use('/api/', limiter);
```

How It Works

- Each client (IP) is allowed **100 requests per 15 minutes**.

- If they exceed the limit, they receive a **429 Too Many Requests** response.

- The `headers: true` option tells clients how many requests remain before hitting the limit.

Fine-Tuning for Different Endpoints

For login routes, you might want even stricter limits:

javascript

```javascript
const loginLimiter = rateLimit({

  windowMs: 10 * 60 * 1000, // 10 minutes

  max: 5, // Max 5 login attempts

  message: 'Too many login attempts. Try again later.',

});

app.post('/login', loginLimiter, (req, res) => {

  // Authentication logic

});
```

This prevents brute-force attacks while still allowing normal traffic.

---

2. Configuring CORS in Express

The Threat: Cross-Origin Restrictions and Security Risks

CORS (Cross-Origin Resource Sharing) determines **which domains can access your API**.

By default, browsers block requests made to **different origins** unless explicitly allowed. Without proper configuration, you might experience:

- **Blocked API calls** in frontend applications.

- **Security risks** from overly permissive policies.

The Fix: Use the cors Middleware

Installing cors

sh

```sh
npm install cors
```

Basic CORS Setup

javascript

```javascript
const cors = require('cors');
```

```
app.use(cors());  //  Allows  all  domains  by
default
```

This setup **enables CORS for all origins**—useful for public APIs, but risky for sensitive data.

Restricting to Specific Origins

To only allow requests from your frontend (`https://myfrontend.com`):

javascript

```
app.use(cors({

  origin: 'https://myfrontend.com',

}));
```

Handling Complex Requests

Some requests—like those with **custom headers** or **credentials**—are considered "preflight" and require extra configuration:

javascript

```
app.use(cors({

  origin: 'https://myfrontend.com',

  methods: 'GET,POST,PUT,DELETE',
```

```
  allowedHeaders:                            'Content-
Type,Authorization',

  credentials: true,

}));
```

- `methods`: Restricts allowed HTTP methods.

- `allowedHeaders`: Specifies which headers clients can send.

- `credentials: true`: Allows cookies and authentication headers.

---

3. Enhancing Security with Helmet

The Threat: Missing HTTP Security Headers

Many Express applications **lack proper security headers**, making them vulnerable to:

- **Clickjacking** (embedding your site in iframes to trick users).

- **XSS attacks** (injecting malicious scripts).

- **Information leaks** (exposing sensitive server details).

The Fix: Use Helmet for Automatic Protection

Helmet **sets up HTTP headers that harden your app against common threats**.

Installing Helmet

sh

```
npm install helmet
```

Basic Helmet Setup

javascript

```
const helmet = require('helmet');

app.use(helmet());
```

This enables a **default set of security headers**, including:

- X-Frame-Options – Prevents clickjacking.

- X-XSS-Protection – Blocks XSS attacks.

- Strict-Transport-Security – Forces HTTPS connections.

Customizing Helmet's Behavior

If you need more control, you can configure specific headers:

430

javascript

```javascript
app.use(
  helmet({
    contentSecurityPolicy: {
      directives: {
        defaultSrc: ["'self'"],
        scriptSrc: ["'self'", 'trusted-cdn.com'],
      },
    },
    referrerPolicy: { policy: 'no-referrer' },
  })
);
```

- contentSecurityPolicy: Prevents unauthorized script execution.

- referrerPolicy: Controls how much referrer information is shared.

Security isn't optional—it's a necessity. By implementing **rate limiting, CORS, and Helmet**, you protect your Express.js application from abuse, unauthorized access, and common security risks.

Key Takeaways

- **Rate limiting** helps prevent brute-force attacks and server overload.

- **CORS** ensures safe cross-origin communication while blocking unauthorized requests.

- **Helmet** applies critical security headers to safeguard against common web vulnerabilities.

As a next step, consider **logging security-related events**, setting up **automated alerts for suspicious activity**, and **monitoring vulnerabilities** using tools like `npm audit`.

By making these security measures part of your standard development process, you'll create **safer, more reliable** applications that can handle real-world traffic and threats.

Chapter 13: Testing Express.js Applications

13.1 Introduction to Testing in Express.js

Let's say you've just built a REST API with Express.js. The routes are working, the database queries return the expected results, and the app runs without errors— at least on your local machine. Confidently, you deploy it to production.

A few days later, bug reports start pouring in:

- A seemingly harmless update broke the user authentication system.

- An API endpoint that worked fine yesterday is now returning incorrect data.

- A new feature conflicts with an existing one, causing unexpected crashes.

Now you're stuck manually debugging, going through logs, and testing routes one by one. **This is exactly what automated testing is designed to prevent.**

Testing is not just about catching bugs; it's about **building confidence in your code.** When you have a solid test suite, you can:

- **Refactor without fear** – You can improve or rewrite parts of your code knowing that existing functionality won't break.

- **Catch regressions early** – If something stops working, your tests will fail before a user notices.

- **Ensure reliability** – A well-tested API is more stable and predictable, reducing unexpected behavior in production.

In modern software development, testing is not an optional step—it's an essential part of writing maintainable, scalable applications.

Different Types of Testing in Express.js

Testing in an Express.js application typically falls into three main categories:

1. Unit Testing – Testing Individual Functions

Unit tests focus on **isolated pieces of code** like utility functions, middleware, or service logic. These tests ensure that small components of your application behave as expected.

For example, if you have a function that hashes passwords, a unit test would verify that it consistently produces the expected output for the same input.

2. Integration Testing – Testing Interactions Between Components

Integration tests check whether different parts of your application **work together correctly.** This might involve testing a route's interaction with a database or ensuring middleware correctly processes requests before they reach the controller.

For instance, an integration test for a login route might:

- Send a request with valid credentials and verify that it returns a valid token.

- Send a request with incorrect credentials and ensure it responds with a 401 error.

3. API Testing – Testing Endpoints and HTTP Responses

Since Express.js is commonly used to build APIs, **API testing is crucial.** This involves sending HTTP requests to your endpoints and verifying that they return the correct status codes, headers, and response bodies.

A common tool for this is **Supertest**, which allows you to simulate real HTTP requests inside your test suite.

What to Test in an Express.js Application

A well-tested Express app covers:

1. Business Logic

- Do your core functions return the expected results?

- Are calculations, data transformations, and conditionals working correctly?

Example: If you have a function that calculates discounts, does it apply the correct percentage under different conditions?

2. API Endpoints

- Do routes return the expected status codes and responses?

- Do they handle valid and invalid inputs properly?

- Do they respect authentication and authorization rules?

3. Middleware

- Does authentication middleware correctly reject unauthorized requests?

- Does input validation middleware catch invalid data before it reaches the controller?

4. Database Operations

- Can your app create, read, update, and delete records as expected?

- Does it handle errors gracefully, such as attempting to delete a non-existent record?

5. Edge Cases and Error Handling

- What happens when an API request is missing required fields?

- How does the app behave when an external service fails?

Covering these areas ensures your app is resilient to unexpected conditions.

Common Testing Tools for Express.js

1. Jest – A Simple and Fast Testing Framework

Jest is one of the most popular testing frameworks for JavaScript. It provides built-in assertions, mocking, and code coverage reporting. It's commonly used for unit tests.

2. Mocha + Chai – A Flexible Alternative

Mocha is a test runner, and Chai is an assertion library. Together, they offer more flexibility than Jest, especially if you prefer writing custom test configurations.

3. Supertest – API Testing Made Easy

Supertest allows you to send HTTP requests to your Express app **without needing to start a real server.** It's ideal for testing API endpoints.

Challenges Developers Face When Writing Tests

"I Don't Have Time to Write Tests"

A common excuse, but in reality, **untested code leads to more debugging time.** Fixing a production issue takes far longer than writing a test to catch it early.

"I Don't Know What to Test"

Start small. Begin by testing utility functions and expand to routes and middleware. A few well-placed tests are better than none.

"Tests Are Breaking, But My Code Works"

If tests fail, don't ignore them—**they're failing for a reason.** Either the test needs updating, or you've introduced unintended behavior.

13.2 Writing Unit Tests with Jest and Mocha

The Developer's Dilemma: Why Unit Testing Matters

Imagine you're working on a new feature in your Express.js application—a function that calculates the total price of items in a shopping cart. It seems straightforward, so you test it manually with a few inputs. Everything looks good. Confidently, you push the code to production.

A day later, a user reports that adding a discount code results in a negative total price. Another user complains that tax calculations are off for orders with multiple items. Now, you're scrambling to debug, stepping through logs and adding console statements to track down the issue.

This is exactly why **unit tests are essential.** They act as a safety net, ensuring that each function in your application behaves correctly, even as you make changes. A well-written unit test would have caught these edge cases before deployment, saving you from production headaches.

In this section, you'll learn how to write effective unit tests for your Express.js applications using **Jest** and **Mocha**, two of the most popular testing frameworks in the JavaScript ecosystem.

What is Unit Testing?

Unit testing is the practice of testing **individual pieces of code**—typically functions or methods—in isolation. The goal is to verify that each unit of code behaves as expected under various conditions.

A unit test should be:

- **Focused** – It tests a single function or module at a time.

- **Isolated** – It does not depend on external systems like databases or APIs.

- **Fast** – It runs quickly, allowing developers to test frequently.

For example, if you have a function that formats a date, a unit test should confirm that it correctly formats different inputs, including edge cases like leap years.

Setting Up Jest for Unit Testing

Installing Jest

Jest is a powerful JavaScript testing framework that includes built-in assertion libraries, mocking capabilities, and test coverage reports.

To install Jest in your Express.js project, run:

sh

```
npm install --save-dev jest
```

Next, add a test script to your `package.json`:

json

```json
"scripts": {
  "test": "jest"
}
```

Now, Jest is ready to run your test files.

Writing Your First Unit Test with Jest

Let's start with a simple function that calculates the total price of items in a shopping cart.

cart.js (Business Logic)

javascript

```javascript
export function calculateTotal(items) {
  if (!Array.isArray(items)) throw new Error("Invalid input");



  return items.reduce((total, item) => {
    if (!item.price || !item.quantity) throw new Error("Missing properties");
    return total + item.price * item.quantity;
  }, 0);
```

```
}
```

Now, let's write a Jest test for this function.

cart.test.js (Unit Test with Jest)

javascript

```javascript
import { calculateTotal } from "./cart.js";

describe("calculateTotal", () => {
  test("calculates total correctly for
multiple items", () => {
    const items = [
      { price: 10, quantity: 2 },
      { price: 5, quantity: 3 }
    ];
    expect(calculateTotal(items)).toBe(35);
  });

  test("returns 0 for an empty cart", () => {
    expect(calculateTotal([])).toBe(0);
```

```
  });


  test("throws an error if input is not an
array", () => {

    expect(()                            =>
calculateTotal(null)).toThrow("Invalid
input");

  });


  test("throws an error if an item is missing
price or quantity", () => {

    const items = [{ price: 10 }];

    expect(()                            =>
calculateTotal(items)).toThrow("Missing
properties");

  });
});
```

Running the Tests

Run the following command in your terminal:

sh

```
npm test
```

Jest will execute the test cases and display a report showing which tests passed or failed.

Using Mocha and Chai for Unit Testing

While Jest is an all-in-one testing framework, **Mocha** provides more flexibility, especially when used with **Chai**, a powerful assertion library.

Installing Mocha and Chai

sh

```
npm install --save-dev mocha chai
```

Modify your `package.json` to include a test script:

json

```
"scripts": {
  "test": "mocha"
}
```

Writing a Unit Test with Mocha and Chai

cart.test.js (Unit Test with Mocha and Chai)

javascript

```javascript
import { expect } from "chai";

import { calculateTotal } from "./cart.js";


describe("calculateTotal", () => {

  it("calculates total correctly for multiple
items", () => {

    const items = [

      { price: 10, quantity: 2 },

      { price: 5, quantity: 3 }

    ];

expect(calculateTotal(items)).to.equal(35);

  });


  it("returns 0 for an empty cart", () => {
```

```
    expect(calculateTotal([])).to.equal(0);

  });


  it("throws an error if input is not an
array", () => {

    expect(()                              =>
calculateTotal(null)).to.throw("Invalid
input");

  });


  it("throws an error if an item is missing
price or quantity", () => {

    const items = [{ price: 10 }];

    expect(()                              =>
calculateTotal(items)).to.throw("Missing
properties");

  });
});
```

Running the Tests

Use the following command to run Mocha tests:

sh

```
npm test
```

Mocha will output the results in a structured format.

Best Practices for Writing Unit Tests

1. **Write Clear and Descriptive Test Names**
   A good test name should describe what is being tested and the expected outcome.

   Good: `"throws an error if input is not an array"`
   Bad: `"test invalid input"`

2. **Test Edge Cases**
   Consider scenarios like:

   - What happens when input values are `null` or `undefined`?

   - How does the function behave with large numbers?

   - Does it handle negative values correctly?

3. **Keep Tests Isolated**
   Unit tests should not rely on databases, APIs, or file systems. If a function depends on an

external service, mock it instead.

4. **Run Tests Frequently**
   Make testing part of your development workflow. Running tests before pushing code helps catch issues early.

Use   Code   Coverage   Tools
With Jest, you can check how much of your code is covered   by   tests:

sh

```
jest --coverage
```

5. This highlights untested parts of your codebase.

13.3 Implementing API Testing with Supertest

Why API Testing is Non-Negotiable

Imagine this: You've just built an API for a to-do list application. You've tested it manually in Postman, sent a few GET and POST requests, and everything seems to be working fine. Confident in your work, you deploy the application.

A day later, a bug report comes in—users are unable to update tasks. You check the logs, manually test again, and everything still looks fine. But then, another issue surfaces: the `DELETE` endpoint is inconsistently failing. At this point, you're stuck in a frustrating cycle—chasing down bugs that could have been caught earlier.

This is why **automated API testing** is crucial. Manual testing may catch obvious issues, but **Supertest**, combined with **Jest or Mocha**, provides a way to automatically verify that your API is working correctly—every single time you make changes. With API testing in place, you can:

- **Catch breaking changes before they reach production.**

- **Ensure endpoints behave consistently across updates.**

- **Save time and effort compared to manual testing.**

By the end of this chapter, you'll learn how to write effective API tests using **Supertest**, validate responses, handle authentication, and apply best practices to make your Express.js applications more reliable.

Getting Started with Supertest

Supertest is a library designed specifically for **testing HTTP servers**. It allows you to send requests to your Express.js API and verify the responses—all within a testing framework like Jest or Mocha.

Installing Supertest

First, install Supertest and your preferred testing framework.

sh

```
npm install --save-dev supertest jest
```

Now, update your `package.json` to include a test script:

json

```
"scripts": {
  "test": "jest"
}
```

With the setup in place, let's write some real API tests.

Writing API Tests for an Express.js Application

Let's assume we have a simple Express API that manages tasks.

Sample Express API (tasks.js)

javascript

```javascript
import express from "express";

const app = express();
app.use(express.json());

let tasks = [{ id: 1, title: "Buy groceries",
completed: false }];

// Get all tasks
app.get("/tasks", (req, res) => {
  res.json(tasks);
});

// Create a new task
app.post("/tasks", (req, res) => {
  const { title } = req.body;
  if (!title) {
```

```javascript
    return    res.status(400).json({    error:
"Title is required" });

  }


  const newTask = { id: tasks.length + 1,
title, completed: false };

  tasks.push(newTask);

  res.status(201).json(newTask);

});


// Update a task

app.put("/tasks/:id", (req, res) => {

  const task = tasks.find(t => t.id ===
parseInt(req.params.id));

  if (!task) {

    return res.status(404).json({ error: "Task
not found" });

  }


  task.completed = req.body.completed !==
undefined ? req.body.completed :
task.completed;
```

```javascript
  res.json(task);

});


// Delete a task

app.delete("/tasks/:id", (req, res) => {

  const taskIndex = tasks.findIndex(t => t.id
=== parseInt(req.params.id));

  if (taskIndex === -1) {

    return res.status(404).json({ error: "Task
not found" });

  }


  tasks.splice(taskIndex, 1);

  res.status(204).send();

});


export default app;
```

Writing API Tests with Supertest and Jest

Now, let's write tests for this API using Supertest.

Setting Up the Test File (tasks.test.js)

Create a `tests` folder and inside it, create a `tasks.test.js` file:

javascript

```javascript
import request from "supertest";

import app from "../tasks.js";


describe("Task API", () => {

  test("GET /tasks - should return a list of tasks", async () => {

    const response = await request(app).get("/tasks").expect(200);


expect(response.body).toEqual(expect.any(Array));

  });
```

```
  test("POST /tasks - should create a new
task", async () => {

    const newTask = { title: "Learn Supertest"
};

    const        response        =        await
request(app).post("/tasks").send(newTask).exp
ect(201);




expect(response.body).toHaveProperty("id");


expect(response.body.title).toBe(newTask.titl
e);


expect(response.body.completed).toBe(false);

  });



  test("POST /tasks - should return 400 if
title is missing", async () => {

    await
request(app).post("/tasks").send({}).expect(4
00);

  });
```

```
    test("PUT  /tasks/:id  -  should  update  a
task", async () => {

    const          response          =          await
request(app).put("/tasks/1").send({
completed: true }).expect(200);


expect(response.body.completed).toBe(true);

    });




    test("PUT /tasks/:id - should return 404 if
task does not exist", async () => {

    await
request(app).put("/tasks/999").send({
completed: true }).expect(404);

    });




    test("DELETE  /tasks/:id  -  should  delete  a
task", async () => {

    await
request(app).delete("/tasks/1").expect(204);

    });
```

```
test("DELETE /tasks/:id - should return 404
if task does not exist", async () => {

    await
request(app).delete("/tasks/999").expect(404)
;

  });

});
```

Running the Tests

Now, execute the tests:

sh

```
npm test
```

Jest will run each test and display the results in a clear format.

Handling Authentication in API Tests

Many APIs require authentication. Supertest makes it easy to include authentication tokens in requests.

If your API uses JWT authentication, you can pass the token like this:

javascript

```javascript
const token = "your-jwt-token-here";

await request(app)

  .get("/tasks")

  .set("Authorization", `Bearer ${token}`)

  .expect(200);
```

If you need to log in before testing protected routes, you can **fetch a token dynamically**:

javascript

```javascript
let token;

beforeAll(async () => {

  const response = await request(app)

    .post("/auth/login")

    .send({ username: "user", password: "password" });


  token = response.body.token;
});
```

This ensures that your tests **always use a valid token** instead of hardcoding it.

Best Practices for API Testing

1. **Test both success and failure cases**

   - Ensure correct responses for valid requests.

   - Verify proper error handling for invalid inputs.

2. **Use descriptive test names**
   Good: `"returns 400 if title is missing in POST /tasks"`
   Bad: `"task post test"`

3. **Keep tests isolated**

   - Each test should be independent and not rely on previous tests.

   - Use **in-memory databases or mocks** instead of modifying a real database.

4. **Test for security vulnerabilities**

   - Check if endpoints are protected from unauthorized access.

- Test for SQL injection or data tampering risks.

5. **Run tests automatically in CI/CD**

- Integrate API tests into your CI/CD pipeline to catch issues before deployment.

PART 5: NEXT STEPS & EXPANDING YOUR KNOWLEDGE

Chapter 14: Scaling Express.js Applications

Why Scaling Matters

Picture this: You've built a robust Express.js API for an e-commerce platform. It started as a simple monolithic application running on a single server. At first, everything worked smoothly, but as more users started making purchases, response times slowed, database queries took longer, and your server struggled to keep up.

Soon, frustrated customers abandoned their carts, complaints flooded in, and the business began losing revenue. Scaling wasn't just an option—it was a necessity.

This is the reality of modern web applications. Whether you're handling thousands or millions of requests per day, scaling ensures your application remains **fast, responsive, and resilient** under heavy traffic.

In this chapter, we'll explore **three key strategies** to scale Express.js applications effectively:

1. **Load balancing and microservices architecture** – Distributing traffic efficiently and breaking down monolithic apps into smaller, scalable services.

2. **Implementing WebSockets** – Managing real-time communication in a scalable way.

3. **Working with serverless frameworks** – Deploying Express.js in a way that auto-scales

with demand.

By the end, you'll have a solid foundation for handling high-traffic applications while keeping performance and reliability at the forefront.

14.1 Load Balancing and Microservices Architecture

Scaling Express.js: Why It Matters

Imagine you've built an Express.js application that starts as a simple monolith. At first, everything runs smoothly on a single server. Your API is responsive, database queries are fast, and users are happy. But as traffic grows, things start to break down. Requests take longer to process, some even time out, and the server crashes under heavy load.

This is the classic scalability problem. A single server has **limited CPU, memory, and network bandwidth**. When it reaches its limits, the application becomes slow and unreliable. If your business depends on this API, every second of downtime could mean lost customers and revenue.

Scaling an Express.js application effectively requires two key approaches:

1. **Load balancing** – Distributing traffic across multiple servers to prevent any single server from becoming overwhelmed.

2. **Microservices architecture** – Breaking a monolithic application into smaller, independently scalable services.

In this section, we'll explore both strategies, providing practical implementation details, best practices, and insights into common pitfalls.

Load Balancing: Distributing Traffic for Reliability

What Is Load Balancing?

Load balancing is the process of **distributing incoming network traffic across multiple backend servers**. Instead of relying on a single machine to handle all requests, a load balancer directs each request to one of many available servers. This ensures that:

- No single server is overwhelmed.

- The system remains responsive even under high traffic.

- If a server fails, traffic can be rerouted to healthy servers, improving reliability.

Types of Load Balancing

There are several common load balancing strategies:

- **Round Robin** – Requests are distributed sequentially among available servers.

- **Least Connections** – Requests are sent to the server with the fewest active connections.

- **IP Hashing** – Requests from the same client are consistently routed to the same backend server.

For most Express.js applications, **Round Robin** is a simple and effective strategy, but in stateful applications (e.g., sessions stored in memory), **IP Hashing** might be preferable.

Setting Up Load Balancing with Nginx

A common approach to load balancing Express.js applications is using **Nginx** as a reverse proxy.

Step 1: Start Multiple Express.js Instances

Run multiple instances of your Express application on different ports:

sh

```
PORT=3001 node server.js &

PORT=3002 node server.js &

PORT=3003 node server.js &
```

Step 2: Configure Nginx as a Load Balancer

Modify the Nginx configuration file (/etc/nginx/nginx.conf):

465

nginx

```
http {

    upstream express_servers {

        server localhost:3001;

        server localhost:3002;

        server localhost:3003;

    }

    server {

        listen 80;

        location / {

            proxy_pass
http://express_servers;

            proxy_set_header Host $host;

            proxy_set_header       X-Real-IP
$remote_addr;

            proxy_set_header   X-Forwarded-For
$proxy_add_x_forwarded_for;

        }

    }

}
```

Step 3: Restart Nginx

sh

```
sudo systemctl restart nginx
```

Now, when clients send requests to port 80, Nginx will distribute them across the three Express.js instances, significantly improving performance and availability.

Breaking the Monolith: Microservices Architecture

Why Move to Microservices?

A **monolithic** Express.js application handles all functionality in a single codebase and server. While easy to start with, it quickly becomes difficult to scale and maintain.

Consider an e-commerce platform. A monolithic Express.js app might include:

- **Authentication Service** – Manages user logins and sessions.

- **Orders Service** – Handles order placement and tracking.

- **Payments Service** – Processes transactions and refunds.

As the application grows, any small change can affect unrelated functionality, deployments become riskier, and scaling is inefficient.

By **breaking the monolith into microservices**, each feature runs as an independent service, allowing:

- **Independent scaling** – Only the services that need more resources are scaled.

- **Faster deployments** – Services can be updated separately without affecting others.

- **Better fault isolation** – If the Orders Service crashes, Authentication and Payments continue running.

Building Microservices with Express.js

Let's refactor our monolithic Express.js app into three microservices:

1. **Auth Service** – Runs on port 4000

2. **Orders Service** – Runs on port 5000

3. **Payments Service** – Runs on port 6000

Each microservice is an independent Express.js app that communicates via **REST APIs** or **message queues (e.g., RabbitMQ, Kafka)**.

Example: Orders Service (orders.js)

javascript

```javascript
import express from "express";

const app = express();
```

```javascript
app.use(express.json());

app.get("/orders", (req, res) => {
    res.json([{ id: 1, item: "Laptop", price:
1200 }]);

});

app.listen(5000, () => console.log("Orders
Service running on port 5000"));
```

Example: Payments Service (payments.js)

javascript

```javascript
import express from "express";

const app = express();

app.use(express.json());

app.post("/pay", (req, res) => {
    res.json({ status: "Payment successful",
transactionId: "abc123" });

});

app.listen(6000, () => console.log("Payments
Service running on port 6000"));
```

Connecting Microservices via API Gateway

Instead of exposing each service directly, we can introduce an **API Gateway** that acts as a central entry point.

Example using **Express.js as an API Gateway**:

javascript

```javascript
import express from "express";

import axios from "axios";



const app = express();



app.get("/orders", async (req, res) => {

    const response = await axios.get("http://localhost:5000/orders");

    res.json(response.data);

});



app.post("/pay", async (req, res) => {

    const response = await axios.post("http://localhost:6000/pay",
req.body);
```

```
      res.json(response.data);

});


app.listen(3000,    ()    =>    console.log("API
Gateway running on port 3000"));
```

Now, clients interact with the **API Gateway**, which routes requests to the appropriate microservice. This improves security and simplifies client interactions.

Challenges and Best Practices

While microservices improve scalability, they introduce new complexities. Here's how to handle them effectively:

- **Service Discovery** – Use a tool like **Consul** or **Kubernetes Service Discovery** to manage dynamically changing service instances.

- **Database Per Service** – Avoid a single shared database; instead, let each service have its own database to prevent tight coupling.

- **Logging and Monitoring** – Use **ELK Stack (Elasticsearch, Logstash, Kibana)** or **Prometheus + Grafana** for centralized logging and monitoring.

- **Resilience Strategies** – Implement **circuit breakers (Hystrix)** and **retry mechanisms** to handle failures gracefully.

14.2 Implementing WebSockets with Express.js

The Need for Real-Time Communication

Imagine you're building a chat application. Users expect instant updates when someone sends a message—without having to refresh the page. Or maybe you're working on a stock market dashboard, where prices should update in real time. Traditional **HTTP requests** just don't cut it in these scenarios.

With HTTP, the client has to repeatedly ask the server, *"Any new messages?"*—a process called **polling**. This is inefficient, wastes resources, and leads to unnecessary delays. A better solution is **WebSockets**, which enable **persistent, bidirectional communication** between the client and the server.

In this chapter, we'll explore how to integrate WebSockets into an Express.js application, understand their inner workings, and implement a real-time chat feature as a practical example.

Understanding WebSockets

How WebSockets Work

WebSockets provide a **full-duplex** communication channel over a single TCP connection. Unlike traditional HTTP requests, which follow a **request-response model**, WebSockets allow the server to send updates to the client **without** waiting for a request.

Here's a high-level breakdown of how a WebSocket connection works:

1. **Handshake** – The client makes an initial WebSocket request using the **ws://** or **wss://** (secure) protocol.

2. **Upgrade** – The server upgrades the connection from HTTP to WebSockets.

3. **Persistent Connection** – Both client and server can send messages anytime.

4. **Closing the Connection** – Either side can close the connection when it's no longer needed.

When to Use WebSockets

WebSockets are ideal for:

- **Chat applications** (real-time messaging)

- **Live notifications** (e.g., sports scores, breaking news)

- **Real-time collaboration tools** (Google Docs-style editing)

- **Stock market updates**

- **Multiplayer online games**

If your app requires **real-time, low-latency updates**, WebSockets are the way to go.

Setting Up WebSockets in Express.js

To enable WebSockets in an Express.js app, we'll use the **ws** library, a lightweight WebSocket implementation for Node.js.

Step 1: Install Dependencies

sh

```
npm install express ws
```

Step 2: Create an Express WebSocket Server

Let's build a simple WebSocket server that allows clients to connect and exchange messages.

javascript

```javascript
import express from "express";
import { WebSocketServer } from "ws";


const app = express();
const port = 3000;


// Create an HTTP server
const server = app.listen(port, () => {
    console.log(`Server       running       on
http://localhost:${port}`);
});


// Attach WebSocket server to the HTTP server
const wss = new WebSocketServer({ server });


wss.on("connection", (ws) => {
    console.log("New client connected");
```

```javascript
// Listen for messages from the client

ws.on("message", (message) => {

    console.log(`Received: ${message}`);

    ws.send(`Server                received:
${message}`);

});


    ws.on("close", () => console.log("Client
disconnected"));

});
```

How It Works

- We create an **Express server** and attach a **WebSocketServer** to it.

- When a client connects, the server logs a message.

- The server listens for messages from the client and responds.

- When the client disconnects, the server logs the event.

Now, let's set up a WebSocket client to interact with this server.

Creating a WebSocket Client

To test the WebSocket connection, create a simple HTML file with JavaScript:

html

```html
<!DOCTYPE html>

<html lang="en">

<head>

    <meta charset="UTF-8">

    <meta                        name="viewport"
content="width=device-width,          initial-
scale=1.0">

    <title>WebSocket Demo</title>

</head>

<body>

    <h1>WebSocket Client</h1>

    <input    type="text"    id="messageInput"
placeholder="Type a message">

    <button
onclick="sendMessage()">Send</button>
```

```html
<ul id="messages"></ul>

<script>
    const ws = new WebSocket("ws://localhost:3000");

    ws.onopen = () => console.log("Connected to WebSocket server");

    ws.onmessage = (event) => {
        const li = document.createElement("li");
        li.textContent = event.data;
        document.getElementById("messages").appendChild(li);
    };

    function sendMessage() {
        const input = document.getElementById("messageInput");
        ws.send(input.value);
```

```
        input.value = "";

    }

  </script>

</body>

</html>
```

How It Works

- The **WebSocket connection** is established when the page loads.

- Messages sent from the input field are sent to the server.

- The server responds, and the message is displayed in the browser.

Try running the Express server and opening this HTML file in your browser. You'll see messages sent in real time.

Enhancing WebSockets: Broadcasting Messages

In many real-world applications, WebSocket messages aren't just sent to one client—they're **broadcasted** to multiple clients.

479

Let's modify our WebSocket server to broadcast messages:

javascript

```javascript
wss.on("connection", (ws) => {

    console.log("New client connected");

    ws.on("message", (message) => {

        console.log(`Received: ${message}`);


        // Broadcast message to all connected clients

        wss.clients.forEach((client) => {

            if    (client.readyState    ===
client.OPEN) {

                client.send(`Broadcast:
${message}`);

            }

        });

    });


    ws.on("close", () => console.log("Client
disconnected"));
```

```
});
```

Now, when a client sends a message, all connected clients will receive it—perfect for chat applications or live notifications.

Error Handling and Debugging WebSockets

WebSockets are great for real-time applications, but they come with potential pitfalls. Here's how to handle common issues:

Handling Connection Errors

Always listen for error events to prevent crashes:

javascript

```javascript
ws.on("error",              (err)              =>
console.error("WebSocket error:", err));
```

Handling Disconnections

WebSocket clients may disconnect unexpectedly. Implement **reconnection logic** in the frontend:

javascript

```javascript
const connectWebSocket = () => {

    const        ws        =        new
WebSocket("ws://localhost:3000");
```

```
    ws.onopen = () => console.log("Connected
to server");

    ws.onclose = () => {

        console.log("Disconnected.
Reconnecting...");

        setTimeout(connectWebSocket, 3000);

    };

    ws.onerror         =         (err)        =>
console.error("WebSocket error:", err);

};

connectWebSocket();
```

This ensures the client reconnects automatically if the connection is lost.

WebSockets vs. Alternatives: When Not to Use WebSockets

While WebSockets are powerful, they aren't always the best choice. Consider alternatives based on your use case:

- **Server-Sent Events (SSE)** – Great for one-way real-time updates, like notifications.

- **Long Polling** – Works for simple applications where WebSockets aren't supported.

- **GraphQL Subscriptions** – Ideal for real-time GraphQL APIs.

If your app requires constant, bidirectional communication, WebSockets are the best choice. Otherwise, simpler solutions like SSE might be enough.

14.3 Working with Serverless Frameworks (AWS Lambda, Firebase Functions)

Why Serverless? The Shift in Application Architecture

Picture this: You've built a simple Express.js API, and everything works great. But as your application grows, you start facing challenges.

- **Scalability becomes an issue**—your server struggles to handle high traffic spikes.

- **Costs rise** because you're paying for server uptime even when your API isn't actively handling requests.

- **Infrastructure maintenance is a hassle**, requiring security patches, monitoring, and load balancing.

This is where **serverless computing** comes in. Instead of running a dedicated Express.js server 24/7, you can deploy your API as **serverless functions** that run **only when needed**. No servers to manage, no scaling headaches—just write your function, deploy it, and let the cloud handle the rest.

In this chapter, we'll explore how to deploy Express.js APIs using **AWS Lambda** and **Firebase Functions**, two of the most popular serverless platforms.

What is Serverless?

The term "serverless" doesn't mean there are no servers—it means **you don't manage them**. Cloud providers like AWS and Google handle provisioning, scaling, and maintenance. Your application runs as small, event-driven functions that execute only when triggered.

Key Benefits of Serverless

- **Automatic Scaling** – Handles high traffic loads effortlessly.

- **Cost-Efficiency** – You only pay for actual execution time, not idle server time.

- **Simplified Maintenance** – No server patching or infrastructure management.

- **Event-Driven Execution** – Functions trigger in response to events like HTTP requests, database changes, or cron jobs.

Common Use Cases for Serverless Express APIs

- **Microservices** – Deploy individual API endpoints as independent functions.

- **RESTful APIs** – Build backend logic without running an always-on server.

- **Webhook Handlers** – Respond to third-party services like Stripe, Twilio, or GitHub.

- **Scheduled Tasks** – Automate jobs like data processing or backups.

Deploying Express.js on AWS Lambda with Serverless Framework

AWS Lambda is Amazon's serverless compute service. By combining it with **API Gateway**, we can turn our Express.js application into a fully serverless API.

Step 1: Install the Serverless Framework

First, install the Serverless Framework globally:

sh

```
npm install -g serverless
```

Then, create a new project and install the required dependencies:

sh

```
mkdir express-lambda && cd express-lambda

npm init -y

npm install express serverless-http
```

Step 2: Set Up Express.js with Serverless

Create an `index.js` file with the following Express setup:

javascript

```
import express from "express";

import serverless from "serverless-http";

const app = express();

app.get("/", (req, res) => {

    res.json({ message: "Hello from AWS
Lambda!" });

});
```

```
export const handler = serverless(app);
```

How it Works:

- We create a simple Express app.

- Instead of running a server, we wrap the app with **serverless-http**, which adapts it for AWS Lambda.

- The function `handler` is what AWS Lambda will execute.

Step 3: Configure Serverless for Deployment

Create a `serverless.yml` file to define your AWS Lambda setup:

yaml

```yaml
service: express-lambda-api

provider:

  name: aws

  runtime: nodejs18.x

  region: us-east-1

functions:

  app:

    handler: index.handler
```

```
    events:

      - http:

          path: /

          method: get
```

Step 4: Deploy to AWS

Run:

sh

```
serverless deploy
```

After deployment, you'll see an endpoint like:

bash

```
https://xyz123.execute-api.us-east-
1.amazonaws.com/dev/
```

Try accessing it in a browser or via **cURL**:

sh

```
curl        https://xyz123.execute-api.us-east-
1.amazonaws.com/dev/
```

Your Express route should return the JSON response.

Deploying Express.js as Firebase Cloud Functions

Firebase Cloud Functions allow you to deploy serverless functions that integrate with Firebase services.

Step 1: Install Firebase CLI

sh

```sh
npm install -g firebase-tools

firebase login
```

Then, initialize a Firebase project:

sh

```sh
firebase init functions
```

Choose **JavaScript** or **TypeScript**, and enable **Cloud Functions for Firebase**.

Step 2: Set Up an Express.js Function

Modify `functions/index.js`:

javascript

```javascript
import express from "express";
```

```
import { onRequest } from "firebase-
functions/v2/https";

const app = express();

app.get("/", (req, res) => {

    res.json({ message: "Hello from Firebase
Functions!" });

});

export const api = onRequest(app);
```

Step 3: Deploy to Firebase

Run:

sh

```
firebase deploy --only functions
```

Once deployed, Firebase provides a URL like:

bash

```
https://us-central1-your-
project.cloudfunctions.net/api
```

You can now access your Express.js API without
managing a server.

Comparing AWS Lambda and Firebase Functions

Feature	AWS Lambda + API Gateway	Firebase Cloud Functions
Best For	Large-scale APIs, enterprise applications	Firebase-based apps, mobile backends
Setup Complexity	Requires AWS IAM roles, API Gateway setup	Easier setup, built into Firebase
Pricing	Pay per request + execution time	Free tier available, but pricing scales with usage
Performance	Slightly better cold start times	Optimized for Firebase ecosystem

Integration	Works with any database or cloud service	Best with Firebase (Firestore, Realtime DB)

Both are great choices, but if you're using Firebase services, **Firebase Functions** will feel more seamless. For general-purpose APIs, **AWS Lambda** provides more flexibility.

Handling Cold Starts and Performance Issues

One drawback of serverless is **cold starts**—a delay when a function is invoked after being idle. Here's how to mitigate it:

1. **Use Warm-Up Functions** – Schedule a CloudWatch cron job (AWS) or Firebase Scheduler to keep functions active.

2. **Optimize Code Execution** – Reduce dependencies and avoid unnecessary computations in function initialization.

3. **Use Provisioned Concurrency** – AWS offers this feature to keep functions warm for predictable performance.

www.ingramcontent.com/pod-product-compliance
Lightning Source LLC
LaVergne TN
LVHW081509050326
832903LV00025B/1422